Learning Activities for Preschool Children

A home teaching handbook for parents

ELLEN B. De FRANCO

With contributions in the learning activities by:

Joyce Costa
Jane Fellman
Nell Mendelson
Joyce Peterson
Jerry Spanos
Maxine Young

Olympus Publishing Company · Salt Lake City, Utah

Two Olympus Plaza, 1670 East Thirteenth South
Salt Lake City, Utah 84105

Manufactured in the United States of America.

ISBN: 0-913420-50-6

Library of Congress Catalog Card Number: 74-29661

Contents

Acknowledgments

This book is an outgrowth of two home teaching programs that were started separately in 1972 by T. H. Bell, then superintendent of the Granite School District (Salt Lake City, Utah) and now Commissioner of Education in the U.S. Office of Education, and Evelyn W. Pickarts, supervisor of parent education for the Los Angeles (California) Unified School District. The two home teaching programs were combined as an experimental demonstration in 1973. The staffs of both programs and the author wish to express appreciation to Dr. Bell and Ms. Pickarts for their inspirational leadership in the planning and implementation of this innovative approach to parent education.

Special thanks are extended to Joyce Costa, Jane Fellman, Carolyn Harron, Nell Mendelson and Maxine Young, of the Los Angeles program, and to Joyce Peterson and Jerry Spanos, of the Granite program.

Appreciation is also extended to Kenneth McClelland, director of the Early Childhood Disadvantaged Parent Project in the Granite School District, whose guidance in the preparation of this book and its companion teacher handbook, has been most helpful.

Ellen B. De Franco

Los Angeles, California
1975

Introduction

Parents have always played games with their children, and most have enjoyed doing it. Recently educators and psychologists who have studied young children carefully have found through research that children learn a great deal from game-type activities. These researchers discovered that infants are even able to respond to simple games. This information is exciting, for it shows that there are many things we as parents can do to help our children learn.

When we play with our children, especially when we use game-type activities such as those in this handbook, we make it easier for them to understand many difficult ideas and concepts. As we help them learn in this way, many good things will happen to them and to us! Not only will we be having pleasant times together, but all of us — particularly our children — will be pleased with their newly acquired information and skills.

Each time a child finds out about something new, he or she is that much better prepared to go to school. In large and small ways, we parents can help our children find that learning and studying are worthwhile. Just think of the important job we can do by teaching our children at home before they are old enough to start going to school. We can help make them eager students early in their lives.

Home teaching is not difficult, and you have already done a lot of it with your child. Don't forget, almost everything your child knows about or knows how to do is something he or she learned at home — probably from you. In order to make your use of the activities (games) pleasant experiences for both you and your child, we have included some suggestions which may be helpful for you to use.

In chapter 1, there are practical ideas for the need for a storage place for materials you will use, ways to introduce games to the child, and things you can do to keep your child interested in the activity. In chapter 2, detailed information is given about the different ways in which a child learns. Included are suggestions for how parents can make it easier for a child to learn, how to judge if the child is learning, and the special skills he or she gets as the learning occurs.

In chapter 3, there is a short introduction on how to watch a child in order to understand him better. This is followed by detailed suggestions for ways to make the activities useful for each child according to the way in which he or she learns best. Chapter 4's activities are divided into four subject categories: language development, sensory motor, science, and mathematics. There are ten basic activities in each category, with additional or more difficult variations of each activity included.

Appendices A and B give additional help, with Appendix A listing titles of books and pamphlets which might be of interest to a parent. These are divided into two categories: (1) parent-child interaction and child development and (2) home teaching how-to-do-it books. Appendix B lists different kinds of materials to use in the activities for little or no cost and places where you might be able to find the materials.

Chapter 1

How to Interest Children in the Activities

Welcome to the home teaching program! You and your family are joining a fast-growing number of satisfied parents and children who have already enjoyed using learning activities (games) together. We are sure you and your children will be pleased, too. We wish you success on this adventure.

The purpose of the games included in this handbook is to help prepare the preschool-age child for kindergarten and elementary school. (These activities can also be used with older children who may be having difficulty with the "three Rs" — reading, 'riting, and 'rithmetic. They are also helpful for adults who have not yet learned to read and write well.)

Although the games are educational, they are not like more formal lessons generally associated with classroom learning. The teachers who helped prepare these activities have worked hard to make them interesting for children. Families who have taken part in home teaching programs have had fun playing these games. This combination of good times and learning is a hard one to beat. A child who discovers early in life that acquiring knowledge can be pleasant will probably be a good student and still like going to school.

You will see that the activities are not hard; on the contrary, some of them may be too easy for your child. If this be so, you may find that the more difficult activities are right for him or her, or you may wish to make up similar activities which will fit your child better. Chapter 3 may prove helpful to you in judging how difficult to make the activities so that your child benefits the most from them.

In the following paragraphs, we have a few suggestions that you may wish to follow. Many times parents have had their own variations of these, also.

Storage Place for Materials

The suggestions below are merely that; if you find that your way of doing things suits your family better, feel free to make innovations.

(1) Set aside a place where you can keep this handbook and all of the materials you will

collect for the activities (see chapter 4 and Appendix B).

(2) Make a special label for the place which will show that it is your child's very own spot. You might want to print his or her name on a piece of paper or cardboard. Use manuscript print (MMMMMMMM or Joan's Bag of Games) for all of your labels, and make the letters large so that your child can see them easily.

(3) Put all of the materials and the handbook together. If possible, use grocery bags or large envelopes for storing items to be used in each activity. For example, you could put all of the number cards and small objects for counting (used in mathematics [1] — "Find Out How Many") in one bag and the ball (for sensory motor [2] — "Fun with Balls") in another.

(4) Label each bag, not only for your own convenience, but also to help the child learn about labels, as suggested in language development (7) — "Name Tag." Before long, you may be happily surprised to discover that your child is able to recognize the labels correctly.

(5) Help your child learn from the beginning to put away the objects for separate games in their own bags or boxes. This will teach the importance of order; it will also make the activities more easily accessible for immediate use.

Introducing the Activities to the Child

(1) Try to decide on a definite time each day to play these games. If you set aside a certain time for these activities, you and your child will get into the habit of the teaching and learning experience. This may be extremely helpful for getting the child accustomed to settling down to concentrating. He will probably look forward to playing the games on a regular basis and may even start reminding you each day as it gets near the time for the activities.

(2) If you cannot set aside a specific time of day for the games, at least try to play them at some time during each day.

(3) The amount of time you devote to the teaching-learning activities will depend upon many things. Our best advice is to try to play the games for as long as your child's interest holds. The longer and more often you both spend on activities, the better learner your child will be.

(4) Whenever possible, choose a quiet spot for the activities. If there are few distractions, your child will find it easier to pay attention to the activities.

(5) Try to make everything as comfortable as you can for both of you. Be sure the light where you work is adequate.

(6) If older children wish to join in the activities, invite them occasionally to do so; but be sure to explain to them that the activities are meant for the younger child and that they must help, not hinder, the child's learning. Tell them that they can act as teachers. Show them what to do so that they can guide the younger child and make the activities pleasant for him.

(7) Explain to your child that you will be playing new games which will help him get ready for school. Show him this handbook and allow him to browse through it. If something catches his eye, you could start with that activity. There is no particular order to the games, but you should always start with the first version of the activity whenever you start a new game. Then as the child progresses, choose the harder versions to match his potential.

(8) Although the activities are ordered in the handbook from easiest to most difficult (that is, language development to mathematics), it is not necessary that you follow this sequence. If your child is not too eager to start a particular activity, it might be wiser to select one that you are fairly sure appeals to him immediately.

Things to Do to Keep the Child Interested

(1) Show enthusiasm about playing the games with your child. If he senses that you are enjoying yourself, he is more apt to have a pleasurable time.

(2) Try to start by suggesting things you know he can do and at which he will have success.

(3) Let him know when he does well or does his best, and compliment him as often as possible.

(4) Encourage your child to tell the rest of the family about what he does. Let everyone else know you are proud of him.

(5) Allow him enough time to work at his own pace and to complete what he starts.

(6) Accept his ideas for doing things as much as you can. Encourage him to experiment.
(7) Show your interest in him by carefully watching and listening to him. Talk to him about what he does as often as you can. This will help him feel good about himself. It will also convince him that what he does has importance.
(8) Be considerate of your child's moods. When and if he seems tired or restless, tell him you can play the games at another time.
(9) Do not force your child to play the games, but be watchful for when he seems ready, such as right after a meal or a nap.
(10) Try not to offer too much to your child at one time. You do not want to confuse him.
(11) Encourage your child to play the games he knows on his own. Make it as easy as possible for him to get the materials he needs from the storage place.

As you play the games over a period of time with your child, you and your family will develop many different ways to use the ideas on the spur of the moment, in all kinds of places. You will find this very convenient, especially on occasions when you and your child have to wait somewhere, as at the doctor's office, for a bus, or whatever.

We hope that whenever and wherever you and your family play learning games such as these, you will find pleasure in using everything around you in an educational way.

Chapter 2

How the Child Learns

The child learns in many ways. Like a sponge, he is constantly soaking up all that occurs about him. He reacts to everything he notices; he picks up new information; he improves on what he can do. Not only does he learn about the world in which he finds himself, but he also gradually learns more about himself — what he can or cannot do. Without effort he stores within his head the many things he has seen and experienced. This stockpile of knowledge can serve him as he finds himself in new situations, helping him relate new ideas to old. How the child learns is truly a miraculous occurrence.

If there are no unusual circumstances which might stand in the way of their learning, all children bring many good traits to learning situations. Probably most important of these is a child's will to learn. This is an inborn trait, for the most part, and is tied in with a child's development. His curiosity is an aid to this drive to learn and it should be treated very carefully. Many children whose curiosity has been dampened lose much of their desire to learn; they become disinterested. For this reason adults do well to always keep in mind how important it is for the young child to be able to satisfy his curiosity as much as possible.

A child's enthusiasm for many things is another valuable quality he brings to the process of learning. He starts life with eagerness about many things, and he is open to the new and different. Often he seems never to tire in his wish to see, to touch, to try out what is around him. This enthusiasm can bubble over in smiles of satisfaction and laughs of pure enjoyment. For some people, such enthusiasm lasts a lifetme.

Another characteristic which helps the child learn is his willingness to try things. Perhaps the fact that he is not self-conscious aids him in this.

Until he has failed, and even sometimes despite that, he shows courage in attempting first-time adventures.

A child's willingness to try again and again helps him learn, too. Who among us adults has not admired a baby as we watched his beginning attempts to stand up? With difficulty he will continue to try, even after hard falls have made him cry in pain. This kind of willingness to try is shown by children on many learning occasions. If the child's interest is kept alive, he will keep right on trying. Perhaps his supply of energy helps him with this.

The combination of all of these traits within a child makes him a good candidate for education. He is always alert and ready to enter into the activities around him if there is nothing in the way to prevent him. He shows that he is ready to be taught. He is eager to explore the new and exciting things around him. He makes it easier for his parents and teachers to teach him in his eagerness to learn.

Theories of the Learning Process

For centuries man has wondered about how the child learns. Today early childhood education is considered extremely important. As a result there is a great deal of research being done on this topic. The findings of Jean Piaget, a Swiss psychologist and educator, have strongly influenced the theories and methods being used throughout the Western world, especially in America. The following discussion on the child's learning experiences is based on an interpretation of Piaget's ideas.

The Child Learns through Experience

The child learns from his experiences, starting with his earliest awarenesses in infancy. All that he perceives or notices through his five senses — seeing, hearing, feeling, smelling, and tasting — feed him information. He becomes aware of what is happening around him. In time he realizes that he himself is a separate being. With more experience, he comes to understand that often there is a relationship between himself and the world about him. For example, Piaget writes that at three and a half months his daughter's foot by chance struck a toy hanging over her crib. This caused it to move and jingle. She took pleasure in this incident. It happened again. From then on she purposely tried to move the toy, having fun with the results each time. In this way she learned more about the toy, about herself, and about the relationship between them.

As the child develops he becomes involved in many different situations from which he can learn. Soon he becomes quick to compare them. He is able to discover differences, similarities, and samenesses among them. In this way he relates one experience to the other and starts to distinguish between them. Each time he encounters something that is new to him, once he understands it, it then becomes something he knows. In other words, he adds the new-found fact to his stockpile of knowledge. As he goes through this process, he is thinking about the new idea; he may even want to talk about it, if he is old enough to speak. He may ask questions about it and tell what it means to him.

When a child notices something which he has never before seen, he will want to touch it. According to his age, he will react in different ways: the infant may just brush it with his hand, or attempt to put it in his mouth; the toddler may grab it, push it, and bang it as he becomes acquainted with it; the slightly older child may examine it closely to determine if it opens, comes apart, or whatever, or he may immediately experiment with it. He may roll or bounce it in his efforts to gain an understanding of it. Most children like to have a close, physical contact with an unfamiliar object. They are eager to make their mark on it in some way, in their efforts to understand its mysteries. An old Chinese proverb fits into this description of how a child learns. It is: "I hear and I forget. I see and I remember. I do and I understand."

Essential Factors Which Enable a Child to Learn

Some of the points which will be included here have already been mentioned in the preceding paragraph. They are repeated here to help the reader know when a child is ready to learn as well as how well he is learning.

Readiness

There are several kinds of readiness, all of which are important. Perhaps the easiest to judge is the child's physical well-being. Certainly if he is tired or hungry he cannot think well. It is harder to judge his emotional readiness. With encouragement, however, often a child who does not want to learn can be persuaded to give it a try. The most important of all readiness concerns that which the child already knows and understands. He will learn best when his parent or teacher is aware of what he knows and what he is able to do.

Attention

The child must be able to pay attention in order to learn. He should be able to watch and listen. Once he is able to pay attention in this way, it will be easier to see how great his interest is. The length of his attention span also shows how much he is interested. A word of warning about a child's attention span (an individual trait that does not always remain the same in a child). Readiness has a lot to do with how long a child can remain attentive as well as how active he is with things that are happening. For example, even very young children who usually go from one thing to another soon can remain fixed in one spot for a fairly long time if they are excited about what they are doing.

Another way to judge a child's ability to pay attention is to notice if there are any distractions around him which could possibly divert him. If he continues what he is doing while ignoring things which usually catch his interest, then it is clear that he is paying attention.

Self-Directed Effort and Perseverance

In order to learn, a child must be willing to work at it. He will accomplish this best by his own efforts. For the child to continue sticking to a task, he needs to realize that he is getting better at understanding and using that which he is trying to learn. Until he gets a feeling of self-confidence in what he is doing, he may not be able to keep trying. At this point the adult who is working with him should praise him whenever she can. It is important to give him approval for his efforts. That approval must be sincere and based on what he really can do. If he is told he is doing well, and he knows that he is not (and he also knows that the adult knows that he is not), he may not want to continue.

Active Involvement

A child who takes part in trying a new idea or skill is more apt to learn it than one who is unwilling to work on it very long. The eagerness with which a child talks about what he is learning, asks questions, and experiments with it shows that he is learning it. He will study the task and discover differences, similarities, and samenesses between it and that which he already knows. He makes it clear that he wants to have firsthand experience with it, whether it be an idea, an object, or a skill to improve. In other words, he pushes himself completely into the center of things.

Repeated Practice

In the act of learning, a child often insists on practicing the new idea or skill again and again. For example, if he has just conquered the art of rolling a ball, he may insist on doing it repeatedly. If he has learned a new word, he may try it out many times. This kind of behavior helps many people learn, both young and old. It combines the need to become better at handling the newly acquired knowledge and to gain the satisfaction of having mastered it. Such practice represents the final step in learning.

How to Make It Easier for a Child to Learn

The best part about teaching the child at home is the fact that there is a fair amount of time one can give to this. In other words, there are more "optional" hours for the parent than there are for the teacher when the child is in school. Even if parents schedule a definite time each day for the learning activities, there may be other times when they decide to do this on the spur of the moment. There may be days, too, when they cannot use the games for some reason. When this occurs, they can make up the lost time later.

As the parent starts to teach the child at home, she may be wondering how much time she should devote to the learning activities. There is no definite amount of time planned because much will depend upon both the parent and the child. Of course, the more time spent, the better; but there is no rule about how much time should be spent. Each parent must decide on how much time she can set aside for home teaching.

In addition to the activities (games), the child will be learning from the parent in the ways that he has from babyhood. For example, everything parents do and say has been teaching and will continue to teach him many things. He learns as he watches and listens. The way the parent washes the dishes, helps him find the seeds in his orange, or answers a question — all of these daily activities put parents in the role of teacher.

An important point for all parents to remember is that it is the *quality* of the time spent with the child that counts, rather than the *amount* of time. For example, if a mother is overtired or is preoccupied with problems, even if she offers her child a great deal of time each day, she may not be able to do the kind of teaching of which she is capable. On the other hand, the mother who is relaxed and enjoys the teaching when she can find spare time between many chores will likely be an effective teacher.

The parent may wish to start by using the activities described in this book. These activities are arranged in sections and organized from simple to more difficult versions. It is hoped, however, that each parent will devise her own variations of the activities. It is also suggested that parents use every opportunity, no matter where they and the child are, to play learning games with him. They will find that it is often possible to do this without any special planning; they can merely take advantage of what is going on at the moment. As they become more experienced in the use of the learning activities, they will discover that they and their child will become clever at improvising.

There are other ways to help the child learn and prepare him for school. Among the most important of these is the use of books and other reading materials. Almost without exception, most children — particularly young children — enjoy being read to, especially before they go to sleep at night. If it is difficult for parents to have books available, they can look at pictures in magazines, on food cans and boxes, or in the newspapers, and then talk with the child about what he sees. It will help him understand that pictures "tell a story," that they can be described with words, and that words help us understand things.

Another good learning activity is to tell stories to the child. Most children become fascinated with storytelling. Suggestions for how to do this are listed in language development (2) — "Stories" in chapter 4.

Whenever possible, it is a good idea to take the child to a library. Often the children's librarian arranges special times for reading to groups of children. She can always offer help to the child in finding books she believes the child will enjoy. The parent should introduce herself and her child to the librarian and encourage the child to seek the librarian's help in selecting a book for himself. The librarian will also be willing to offer many ideas on new books or most suitable books for the parent to read to the child.

Television is yet another source of learning and can be used to great advantage, if it is used wisely. For the child to get the most from viewing television, the number of hours he watches should be limited. The purpose of this is to prevent him from becoming so accustomed to television that he will not want to try other things and will become mentally lazy from watching too much television. After the parent and child have agreed on the amount of time he may watch each day, and he has decided on his favorite programs, they should watch together. Afterwards, the parent should talk to him about what he has seen. This can be a good learning experience for him. He should be asked to tell what he has seen, his understanding of it, how he feels about it. He should be encouraged to tell the order of events; what were the reasons, in his opinion, that certain things took place, and what effect did they have? He should be helped to think about answers to problems by being asked such questions as: "If the boy hadn't fed the dog, what do you suppose might happen to the dog?" The parent could suggest that the child pretend to be one of the characters — to play-act the character in his own way or to make up a story different from the one he saw on television.

Whenever possible, the child should see the many worthwhile programs and specials which are made just for children or family viewing. Television can provide a treasure chest of learning for the child (and the parent, too) if programs are chosen with care.

What Parents Can Do to Help

The following is an outline of some of the things that can be done to set the stage for the child's learning. (Most parents probably do all or some of these things already. If so, this will help convince you that you are capable to do home teaching. You will note also that some of these ideas have already been mentioned in other sections of this book. The reason they are repeated several times is because of the valuable part they play in the process of learning.)

The first, and continually best thing parents can do for their child is to help him gain confidence in everything he does. Every kind of support they give him will help him get ready to try new things, no matter what they are. This can best be done if parents look for chances to show their approval of him and what he does. Often just a smile will carry the message to him that a parent is pleased. To be certain that he knows when his actions are approved, however, it is wise to tell him this. As parents and teachers, we are more apt to criticize or show disapproval than we are to praise. For this reason it never hurts to mention when the child is doing well. It is equally important to hold back on criticism. If it is really needed, words that will encourage him rather than discourage him should be used. For example, "How about trying another way to do it?" is better than saying "You did it all wrong!"

Another way to build confidence in a child is to give him many chances to do things at which he can succeed. Often this takes some thinking and preplanning on the part of the parent, but it is well worth the effort because it usually can help improve the child's self-image. As he begins to like himself better and becomes more certain of what he can do, his self-esteem will grow.

An important part of learning has to do with allowing a child to explore and experiment on his own. This is very necessary. Once parents have checked to be sure of the child's safety, then letting him discover on his own is helpful. If he has enough time to proceed at his own pace, this will make learning easier for him. Whenever the child becomes interested in something unusual, if parents can let him study it until his curiosity is satisfied, he will also learn better.

Generally adults are quick to cut short a child's ideas in their eagerness to tell or show him something. It is better to encourage him to talk about his own thoughts. This helps him tackle the new learning by thinking, adapting it to what he already knows, and seeing its relationship to other things. All of these steps are those he must take in order to understand the learning and make it meaningful to him. The more he is able to work things through with the use of his own ideas, the better a learner he becomes.

As parents watch and listen to him, they can be gathering ideas as to what their child does or does not understand. Such information will make it easier for them to suggest things to him if he needs help. For example, he may say something which shows that his thinking is wrong. At this point the parent can correct him, and so remove stumbling blocks from his path of learning.

The more ideas a parent has for offering her child many ways to think about something new, the more she is helping him more clearly understand its meaning. For example, if a mother is helping the child learn the number "two," she can find many things of which there are two, or a pair: eyes, ears, arms, faucets in the bathroom basin, headlights on cars, shoes, stop signs at each side of an intersection, armholes in a jacket, and so forth. Each additional pair of two will make it easier for him to understand "two."

A child is able to learn best when he has many chances to use things in his own way. When he is faced with new objects or materials, he may first imitate how others use it. In time, however, he will want to arrange things according to his own skills and experiment according to his own plans. By so doing, he will be performing many learning roles: as a discoverer, in his attempts to predict what will happen and then make it happen through what he does; as a creator, in the way he moves things about in his own special way and organizes their total pattern; as an inventor, in the often unexpected results of the mixing of two objects which turn out to be so different from what they were first; as an engineer, in the way he works to make something which will serve him later as a tool. The worlds he can conquer, the big push to learn he can experience, these and many more benefits can come to the child if he is given as many chances as possible for doing things by himself.

How to Judge if the Child Is Learning

Often parents and teachers take for granted that children have understood what they have been taught. Frequently we are satisfied if the child answers "yes" to our question of whether he has understood. But such an answer from the child does not always mean that he has understood. He may be embarrassed or afraid to say that he has not understood. He may be tired of learning, therefore he grabs at the opportunity to stop working. It is wise therefore for the parent to try to decide if the child is learning.

There are several ways to do this. Perhaps one of the best clues which shows a child is learning is if his interest lasts. This applies both to the time a parent is working with him and later on. If he talks about what he has been learning or wants to play the game again, or afterward if he mentions that he has thought of something that relates to what he has just learned, then the parent can be sure the new information has been meaningful to him. He is making it a part of his inventory of knowledge.

Another way in which a child shows that he has thoroughly learned something is when he mentions it at another time, in relation to new learning. If he asks questions such as: "If the magnet doesn't pick up this leaf, does it mean that the leaf isn't heavy enough to sink — like the piece of wood that we soaked ahead of time did when we played 'floating objects'?" the parent can be certain he understood the game about finding out which objects float and which sink. Concerning the game he is now playing — his attempts to make comparisons to what he already knows, and to relate them to other experiences, proves he is also learning now. His behavior shows that he has learned how to learn and that learning presents a challenge he is willing to meet.

It is necessary to keep in mind, however, that a child's ability to learn is not always the same. He will have his bad as well as his good days. Often he may forget today what he seemed to know perfectly yesterday. If he shows his interest in the ways outlined above for most of the time, however, the parent can assume correctly that he is learning much, if not all, of what he is being taught.

Special Skills Achieved in Learning

When parents play learning games with their child or talk with him about any learning experience, they are helping him improve special skills which will be of use to him throughout his life. In a way, they are making it possible for him to learn to think clearly and logically. As he gets more practice, these skills will become fairly automatic for him. He will be able to use them easily to his great advantage. The following list includes some of these special skills:

(1) *Alertness:* The more a child's curiosity about his world is satisfied by learning new facts, the more alert he will become to everything about him. He will have enthusiasm and will usually be on his "mental toes" to notice what is going on.

(2) *Observation:* With experience, a child can discover useful ways of studying and looking at things. He will concern himself with significant details. He will look for many properties in one object such as, for example, noting size, shape, weight, height, breadth, surface texture, color, and so forth. He will adapt a scientific approach.

(3) *Questioning:* The more a child raises questions, the clearer his thinking can become and the better the chances will be that his conclusions are correct. As he thinks about the "why's" of things, about cause and effect, as he wonders, "What will happen if . . . ," he is taking on the role of an explorer. His ability to be open-minded, and his willingness to look at one situation from many angles will always be a useful trait for him to have.

(4) *Awareness:* The ability to notice things and be aware of everything about him helps a child think clearly. As he realizes that things can be seen in their entirety and also according to their separate parts, he has conquered a difficult thought process. For example, when he has learned the individual numbers "one" to "ten," if he can recognize all of them as belonging to his set of numerals one to ten, he is aware of the parts which go into creating the whole — in this case, the set. Another example might concern his ability to recognize a wheel as a part of a truck, or the rim of the wheel as a part of the wheel itself.

(5) *Problem solving:* The more the child considers every aspect of a situation, the better he becomes at looking below the surface of everything, including the way people behave. As he searches for the reasons things are as they are, or tries to figure out the possible answers to puzzling problems, he is learning not to accept things at face value. He is sharpening his thinking tools. An example of this is in the way a child might discuss the top of a coffee pot. He will figure out how it fits over the rest of the pot. He will reason that if it is not in place when one starts to make the coffee, the water in the pot will spill out, and the source of the heat (gas, wood, even electricity) may be put out. He will be looking at all possibilities in one situation.

(6) *Adaptability:* As the child has success in using all of his special learning skills, he will be able to adjust to change. The self-confidence he has gained in his learning achievements will give him the courage to attempt almost anything that catches his interest or that the parent encourages him to try. This adaptability will make it possible for him to try a variety of approaches to new situations.

Chapter 3

Adapting Activities to the Individual Child

For a child to learn in the most meaningful way, it is necessary that you observe him and listen to him so that you can determine:

(1) His ability to understand
(2) How easily he learns new things
(3) How well he accepts and follows directions
(4) How well he expresses his feelings, ideas, and desires
(5) How well he can concentrate; whether he is easily distracted
(6) The length of his usual attention span
(7) What he already knows
(8) What his interests are
(9) How much help he needs and in what areas
(10) How much he tries to do things in his own way
(11) How independently he can work
(12) How often he needs a change of pace
(13) How often he needs new ideas to remain interested
(14) How patient he can be
(15) How long he can persevere at a difficult task
(16) How much frustration he can tolerate

Although a child may occasionally vary in all of the above in time, under ordinary circumstances, you should be able to see an overall pattern in his behavior. Once you are more familiar with this, you can plan for him accordingly. Through trial and error, you will also discover:

(1) How much enthusiasm he has for learning
(2) The kinds of games he likes best or likes least
(3) The times of the day he works best and under which conditions
(4) How confident he is about starting new activities
(5) How much he likes to repeat activities
(6) How imaginative he is in making up his own variations of the activities (games)

Each child will react differently; each parent and teacher will show a variation in teaching styles; and each learning experience will have its unique quality. Because of all of these variables, it is impossible to set up definite directions on how to proceed. The following are samples of what you can do to vary the suggested activities shown in chapter 4. We have chosen mathematics (10) — "Length" as an example.

1. **Relation of new ideas to what child already knows:**

   a. Talk with the child to find out his understanding of the word "tall."
   b. Encourage him to consider whether he is as tall as you, as tall as his sister, and so forth.
   c. Stand beside the child before a full-length mirror.
   d. Ask him to put his hand on top of his head.
   e. Maintaining same height, move his hand over his head to where it reaches on you.
   f. Explain that this is the way to compare who is taller.
   g. Now he is able to see and compare, through viewing your heights as well as through experience of his hand measurement, where the top of his head reaches on you.
   h. Ask the child to discuss who is tall and who is short in family by how he sees them.
   i. Continue with the remainder of the steps of the activity (as outlined in chapter 4).

2. **Pace of presentation:**

   If the child is restless —

   a. Vary kinds of activities, from quiet to active. For example, after a brief discussion of who is tall (and so on), let the child climb onto a chair to help measure heights of family members.
   b. In every possible way, allow him to become physically involved with what is occurring.
   c. Limit the amount of quiet activities, such as looking at pictures, until he seems ready to proceed to the active parts of the game.
   d. Give him a measuring stick or a ruler and tell him to go round the room and through the house, measuring everything he sees.

   If the child is very interested —

   e. Continue with the presentation and its variations as outlined, so long as he remains absorbed and you have time to work with him.

3. **Amount of repetition, review, or variation on one concept:**

   If the child learns easily —

   a. Introduce new vocabulary words more rapidly.
   b. Involve him in more comparisons of heights of people and objects.
   c. Help him work on his own body measurements, using his body, his reflection in mirror, or his silhouette cut from paper.
   d. Proceed to more difficult activities as fast as he can learn them.

   If the child learns slowly —

   e. Use the first part of the activity only.
   f. Repeat the height measurements of family members until he seems to understand the comparisons.
   g. Talk about these comparisons as much as possible.
   h. Review comparisons with him the following day.
   i. Cut two string lengths for him to use for comparison.
   j. Gradually add another string length, and another, until he can identify each.
   k. Take cues from the child to decide his readiness for each variation of the activity.
   l. Occasionally reintroduce the activity or one of its variations to see how much learning the child has retained.

4. **Adjustment to the child's ability to concentrate:**

   If he is easily distractible —

   a. Try to find a quiet spot in which to present activities.
   b. Plan to introduce the child to an activity in short, easy steps. For example, ask him to look at family members in a mirror; briefly discuss comparisons of heights. At another time, mark height measurements on a closet door; discuss. Still later, measure the marked measurements; discuss.
   c. Do not force the child to be attentive when he becomes disinterested or restless.

   If he is able to concentrate for a long period of time —

   d. Allow him to experiment with each step and variation of an activity for as long as his interest holds.
   e. Give him as many different books (and the

like) as you can; choose books with pictures of people in them.

f. Encourage him to measure and compare heights in all appropriate pictures.

g. Make his and as many other body silhouette cutouts as you can for him to measure and compare.

Adapting to the Child's Interests

The longer you play the games (activities) with the child, the better you will be able to observe which kinds of activities — and perhaps which of the four categories (found in chapter 4) — intrigue him the most. Use this information to try to make up other similar activities. Do all you can to make each variation a little harder for him so that the activities will continue to challenge him. Take advantage of the child's favorite activities by planning to use them from time to time to:

(1) Get the child in the mood for working on new activities with you
(2) Reward the child for working hard
(3) Amuse the child if he is ill
(4) Review

Considering the Child's Environment

If the child's surroundings and family life offer him opportunities for learning many things, plan to incorporate whatever you find in his immediate environment. For example, if his father is a cabinetmaker who works at home, use every chance you find to have the child observe how his father plans his work and what his father is doing — what tools he is using. You can use such experiences with the following activities:

Category	*Number*	*Title*	*Purpose*
Language development	(3)	Correct Reasoning	Observation, logical thinking
	(5)	Verbal Description	Practice in verbally describing objects
	(7)	Labeling	Recognition of pictured or written labels (on supplies, tools, and the like)
	(9)	Characteristics	Perception of characteristics of things
	(10)	Learning Trips	Exposure to new things and experiences
Sensory motor	(4)	Spatial Awareness	Awareness of position
	(6)	Right and Left	Right and left directions
	(7)	Sense of Hearing	Differentiation of sounds (sawing, planing, nailing, and so forth)
	(8)	Sense of Smell	Differentiation of odors (wood, sawdust, glue, and so on)
	(9)	Surface Texture	Texture differences (wood, metal hinges, sandpaper, and so on)
Science	(6)	Tools	Tools and their use

Mathematics	(1)	Number Concepts	The numbers "one" to "ten"
	(3)	Ordinal Sequence	Ordinal names of activities that take place in an orderly fashion (first he measures; second, he saws; third, he nails; and so forth)
	(4)	Comparison of Number Amounts	More than and less than (parts of a whole, and so on)
	(6)	Geometric Shapes	Recognition of shapes
	(10)	Length	Length measurements

If a child's home environment gives him little or no chance for exposure to new ideas, materials, and experiences, try to show him a variety of picture books, and read to him as much as possible. As you learn what seems to interest him the most, try to increase his understanding and learning in these areas by being more selective about the books you bring to show him. In this way you will be offering him more concepts to think about and learn. This will help him at a later time when he is a student in school.

Chapter 4

Activities

The following activities have been adapted from those used successfully by the teachers in the home teaching programs in the Los Angeles Unified School District and the Granite School District. They have been organized into four categories: language development, sensory motor, science, and mathematics. There is no particular order in the activities in each of the four section — they have been selected at random and offer a variety of learning opportunities for the child. You will find that many important concepts are missing. For example, two of the five senses were omitted in the sensory motor section. Space limitations account for these omissions.

You will notice that each activity, and the additional or more difficult versions of it, concerns only one aspect of learning. In other words, the activities are not intended to be all-inclusive; they do not represent every step necessary for a total understanding of other related concepts. For example, mathematics (9) — "Relationship of Size to Volume" deals with that relationship only and does not mention the concept of measuring amounts (such as spoonful, cupful, pint, and so forth). Nor is the act of measuring stressed in science (5) — "Cooking," for this activity concerns only the changes that occur when raw food is cooked.

Our purpose in presenting these activities in this relatively simple way is to permit the child to understand one idea as thoroughly as possible before he tackles a series of related concepts. Once the child has mastered one idea, he is in a better position to accept a related or more difficult one. His ability and willingness to learn can be strengthened when he is not asked to try too much at one time. If the learning experience is kept uncluttered, the child will respond much more enthusiastically than if he is asked to try to comprehend too many different things at one time.

In chapter 3 suggestions were made for the adaptation of the activities to meet the needs of individual children. It is hoped that the approximately 190 activities herein will be useful in themselves, but whenever possible, parents and teachers are urged to create their own versions to suit the child with whom they are working. Some children may need a great amount of practice with these activities; others may quickly learn from them and thus require more difficult activities. In Appendix A, you will find titles of books which have learning activities suitable for use with young children.

It is our opinion that the most important of all the activities included in this book is language development (2) — "Stories." In the true sense of the word, "Stories" is not an activity per se, but more a family custom. The more a child is read to and the more opportunities he has to look at, handle, and talk about books, the better prepared he is to understand how valuable books are as sources of learning. Research has shown, too, that the children who have enjoyed books in their preschool years are usually those who learn to read and write more easily than the children who have not had such experience with books before they enter elementary school.

Language Development

Suggested age range: Four to five years

(1) Sound Patterns

Listen for Sound-Alikes

Purpose: To help the child hear differences and similarities between spoken sounds and sound patterns

Concepts

1. Everything spoken has a sound or sound pattern.
2. Many of these sounds and patterns sound alike.

Skills

1. Ability to listen carefully
2. Ability to hear differences and similarities in sound and sound patterns
3. Imitation of sound and sound patterns
4. Ability to rhyme

Vocabulary

sound	alike	beginning sounds
sound patterns	different	rhyme

Materials Needed	*Suggested Activities*
Anything at hand	1. Ask the child to listen as you give two short taps — with your fingernail or a pencil, spoon, or twig — first to one and then to a different object. (Be sure that each of the taps makes a different sound.) Ask her if the sounds are alike or different. Discuss the differences.
	2. Suggest that the child tap two additional objects in the same manner.
	3. Encourage the child to continue this tapping experiment so that she can listen for sounds that are alike and different.
	4. When she understands the concept of alike and different sounds, switch to using the words by starting with her name and one that sounds like it (Ann and Nan; Carmen and Norman).
	5. Say a name that is different (Ann and Rose; Carmen and Danny). Play this game with her by using the names of people she knows.

Additional or More Difficult Activities

1. Which sounds different?
   a. Use simple words with which the child is familiar. Say sets of three (hat, cat, lid).
   b. Use longer words (doing, stewing, nailing).
   c. Ask the child to think of more words that are alike and different.

2. Beginning sounds
   a. Copy activities above, but ask the child to listen especially for the beginning sounds which are alike or different (baby, ball, sock).
   b. Ask the child to find more words for this activity (game).
   c. Ask the child to find pictures of objects whose names sound alike. Talk about these with her. Cut out the pictures, mix them up, add a few more she has not seen. Ask her to sort them into sets that are alike and different.

   Old magazines and newspapers; large envelop for storage

   d. Repeat this activity with the child every day, adding new pictures so that she can practice.

3. In my suitcase
   a. Tell the child, "I am going to take a trip. In my suitcase I'll put my *shoes*." Ask her to think of something with the same beginning sound (socks). Continue this activity, allowing the child to decide on the first word every other time.

4. Making rhymes
   a. Teach the child a simple, short rhyme ("Rain, rain, go away. Come again another day"). Explain that words which rhyme sound alike.
   b. Try to think of words that sound alike and make funny, short word-rhymes (silly Billy; hum with gum). Ask the child to make up similar word-rhymes.
   c. Make up short rhymes about things familiar to the child ("Tip, our cat, is so fat"). Encourage the child to make rhymes.

5. Homemade rhymes book

   Paper, paper bags, or wrapping paper; hole puncher; yarn or string; pen, pencil, crayon, or felt pen

   a. Make a scrapbook.
   b. As the child composes rhymes, print them in the scrapbook. If she likes to draw, she may wish to "illustrate" the book.
   c. The scrapbook serves a twofold purpose: It will help keep the child interested in spoken sound patterns, and later, when she starts to read, she will enjoy reading the scrapbook.

Suggested age range: Two to five years

(2) Stories

Story Time

Purpose: To involve the child in listening to, thinking about, and discussing stories, and to improve his understanding and use of language

Concept: Stories offer information, ideas, and entertainment.

Skills

1. Ability to listen
2. Ability to think and understand meanings of stories and people's behavior
3. Ability to understand proper sequence of events
4. Ability to create own stories

Vocabulary

plot	real	make believe
after	before	first
next	last	plays

Materials Needed	*Suggested Activities*
Children's picture books	1. Select a book that you believe will interest the child. Start with a short book. 2. Read the book to yourself; this will make it easier to read aloud to the child. 3. Be sure that the child is comfortable and prepared to sit quietly. 4. Expain to the child that you will read the entire book and that afterwards he can look at the pictures and talk about the story. 5. Read the entire story to him. 6. Encourage the child to look at the pictures and discuss how they relate to the story. 7. Listen to what he says so that you learn his understanding of the story.

8. Ask the child questions about the characters and the events in the story.
9. Find out if the child understands the sequence of events by asking such questions as, "After the boy went out, what happened?"
10. Ask the child questions about the meaning of the plot and relationship between cause and effect: "Why do you think the boy went out?"
11. Ask the child questions about how he thinks characters might feel: "Does he look sad or happy? Why do you think she is crying?"
12. Encourage the child to retell or "read" the story.
13. Suggest that he make up his own ending to the story, or tell you a story that he makes up himself.

Additional or More Difficult Activities

1. Storytelling
   a. Tell the child stories — those you know and those you make up.
   b. Try to adjust the length of the story to the amount of time the child's interest will hold.
   c. Be as dramatic as possible. Change the volume and tone of your voice as much as you can. Use gestures and facial exaggerations to help illustrate your tale.
   d. Talk about the story with the child after you have told it. Ask him the same kinds of questions as suggested in the earlier steps of suggested activities.
   e. Encourage the child to retell your story or to make one up by himself.

Books, magazines, newspapers; pictures on billboards or posters; scenes from television shows

2. What happened here?
   a. Show the child a picture of people or animals.
   b. Ask the child to think about what might have occurred or what could happen to the people or the animals.
   c. Help the child make up a story about the picture.

Yours and the child's fingers; crayons and felt pens; fabric and paper scraps; paper bags; cardboard tubes; old socks or mittens; popsicle sticks or tongue depressor; needle, strong thread, yarn; scissors; paste or glue; spools, walnut shells, acorns, and the like

3. Story plays
   a. Make simple puppets from any of the listed materials. Be sure that the puppets are easy for the child to use (make hand puppets small enough to fit child's hand). Attach all parts of the puppet firmly together.
   b. Reenact a familiar story, or make one up, using puppets.
   c. Encourage the child to work a puppet as you tell a story.
   d. Ask him to make up his own puppet plays.

Puppets of all kinds

Suggested age range: Three and a half to five years

(3) Correct Reasoning Thinking Cap

Purpose: To help the child think logically and organize her thoughts into words

Concept: It is possible to reason about people's behavior and about events.

Skills

1. Observation
2. Ability to raise relevant questions
3. Organization of thoughts and speech

Vocabulary

right	wrong	figure out
problem	sensible	logical

Suggested Activities

---

1. First, ask the child to think and talk about why she does such things as eat, sleep, play, and watch television.
2. Next, when you ask the child to do something, talk over with her the reasons for your request.
3. When something happens and you do something about it, explain to the child why you do it (such as closing a window when it starts to rain).
4. As you do things, ask the child if she knows the reason for your actions ("Why do you think I watered the plants?").
5. Ask her to explain why she thinks:
   a. Babies take a nap after lunch.
   b. Mothers and fathers work.
   c. People wear shoes.
6. Make up simple situations as samples below and ask the child to explain them:
   a. Tom plays outside with Jim every day. Today it is raining, and Jim is sick. Today Tom plays alone in his house.

b. Daddy just got into his truck. He is not able to start the motor. The truck keys are still on the kitchen table.
c. The bread in the toaster is not turning brown. The switch on the toaster works. The toaster is not plugged into the wall socket.

7. Encourage the child to reason about everything that she notices happening around her.

8. Watch the programs the child watches on television, and ask her to talk about the *why's* of behavior and events.

Additional or More Difficult Activities

1. Which makes sense?
   a. Make up a series of three of four solutions to situations the child can understand. Ask her to select the most sensible one. For example: Mary's doll is on a shelf too high for her to reach. Which is the best way for her to get it?
      (1) Ask her little sister to reach it.
      (2) Phone her father at work.
      (3) Pull up a chair and get it herself.

2. What comes next?
   a. Tell the child to think of suitable endings to sentences such as:
      (1) The traffic light turned red, so the cars . . .
      (2) My feet are wet, so . . .
      (3) The fork is dirty, so . . .

3. What should I do?
   a. Ask the child to supply reasonable solutions to problems which can be stated in one sentence, such as:
      (1) I forgot one mitten and my hands are cold.
      (2) I am not hungry, but I am thirsty.
      (3) My baby sister is crying.

4. Every time the child has a problem, ask her to try to solve it through reasoning as she did in these activities.

Suggested age range: Three and a half
to five years

(4) Finding Clues

Detective

Purpose: To sharpen the child's awareness of clues

Concepts

1. Clues can be used to discover information.
2. The use of clues may help to solve problems.

Skills

1. Observation
2. Ability to follow clues
3. Determination of the usefulness of clues

Vocabulary

clue   riddle   solve

Materials Needed	*Suggested Activities*
	1. Explain to the child how clues are used to discover things (a dry mouth is a clue that the person is thirsty).
	2. Ask the child to tell you what the following clues tell: a. Yawning child (sleepiness) b. Meowing cat (hunger) c. Distant thunder (a storm is coming)
A "feel box" (described in sensory motor (9) — "Surface Texture")	3. Ask the child to put his hand into the "feel box" and, as he handles an object, tell which clues he feels indicate the object's identity (the ball is round, hard, and so on).
	4. Set up situations when the child is not looking, with visible clues for him to find: a. Tilt (clue) fruit bowl and spill fruit onto table. Leave bowl in tilted position. b. Unplug cord (clue) from electric clock. Tell the child that the clock has stopped.

c. Remove a small picture from the wall, and remove nail (or tack) on which it had hung. Put the nail on the floor also.

Additional or More Difficult Activities

Picture books or magazines

1. What are the clues?
   a. Look at pictures with the child. Ask him to describe what the pictures show and what clues in them help him understand them.

Old magazines, catalogs, or newspapers; scissors; construction paper; paste; large envelope

   b. Cut out pictures of objects and scenes and paste them on construction paper.
   c. Put pictures in the envelope. Pull out a small portion of one picture. Ask the child to guess what the object (or scene) is from the clue you are showing him.
   d. Add new pictures from time to time and repeat this activity often.

Paper; scissors; books or magazines

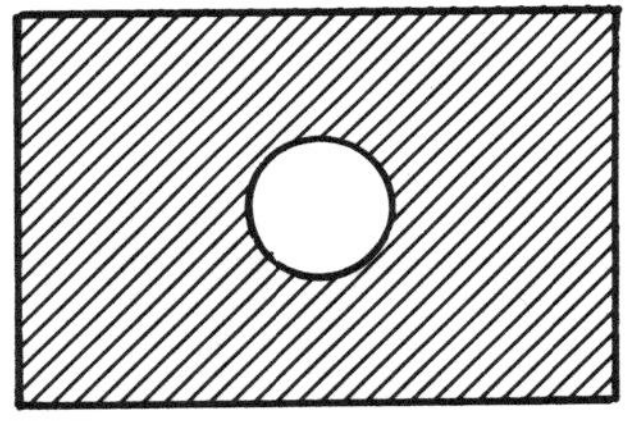

Screen frame

2. Clues in the hole
   a. Make a small screen frame by cutting a hole in the middle of the paper about eight by eight inches.
   b. Find pictures the child has not seen before. Place the screen frame over a picture and ask the child to tell you what he thinks the picture shows, taking his clues from part of the picture which he can see through the hole.
3. Figure this out
   a. Riddles supply spoken clues for solving problems. Find easy ones in a book, or make up riddles:
      (1) No matter how hot or cold it is, what melts when you take it out of its usual storage place? (Answer: ice cream, butter, ice, and so on.)
      (2) What is alive, makes noises, is soft, but has no fingers? (Answer: cat, dog, lamb, and so on.)
4. Clues everywhere
   a. Encourage the child to be constantly alert to clues everywhere, such as:
      (1) A crocus pushing up through the snow is a clue that spring will soon arrive.
      (2) The sound of running water in the pipes is a clue that Daddy is watering the flowers.
      (3) The baseball bat on the chair is a clue that brother is home.

Suggested age range: Three and a half to five years

(5) Verbal Description — Talk Diary

Purpose: To give the child practice in verbal description

Concepts
1. There is a logic in the way things are made, organized, and arranged.
2. There are practical reasons for the way we organize what we do.

Skills
1. Organization of thoughts
2. Awareness of sequence of events
3. Spoken description
4. Observation

Vocabulary

order	first	then
next	after	diary
reported		

Materials Needed	*Suggested Activities*

---

1. Explain to the child what a dairy is, and tell her you will help her keep a "Talk Dairy."
2. Encourage her to talk to you about everything she has done since she got out of bed this morning.
3. Help her organize the order in which she did things, asking such questions as:
   a. What did you do first?
   b. What happened next?
   c. After that, where did you go?
4. Occasionally, try to trick her by reordering the sequence of events, such as: "Did you put your pajamas on to go out to play?" The more humorous you make these questions, the better she will like them.

5. Ask her to give a "Talk Diary" of what you have been doing all day since you got up. Help her out if she cannot recall everything, or if she was not with you all of the time.
6. Ask her to practice giving Talk Diaries of everyone in the family — her pet(s), stuffed animals, imaginary companions, friends, and so on.

Additional or More Difficult Activities

1. Reporter
   a. Explain to the child what a reporter is. Ask her to pretend she is one by talking about everything that is happening around her as it occurs. For example, if you are cooking supper, she is helping you, brother is doing his homework, sister is putting rollers in her hair, ask the child to describe everything.

Old magazines, catalogs, newspapers, picture books, pictures already cut out for other activities; scissors

2. The why's and what's
   a. Using a picture of one subject (a shoe), talk with the child about it in detail. For example, raise questions about why we wear shoes, of what they are made, what different kinds there are, how we put them on, and so on.
3. The where
   a. Cut out pictures of furniture and house furnishings. Ask the child to sort them according to which room they belong. Next, ask her to take one room's furnishings and arrange them in approximately the same position as the real objects are in the home.
   b. As she places them, ask her to talk to you about why she thinks they go in certain spots.

Paper; paste

   c. If she enjoys this activity, suggest that she paste the room arrangements in a scrapbook.
4. How to do it
   a. As the child does something that she customarily does, ask her to describe the steps she takes to complete the task. For example, if she is able to put on her own socks, encourage her to talk about exactly what she is doing as she is doing it.
5. Walk-talk
   a. When you go outside for a walk, ask the child to tell you about everything she does, sees, hears, smells, touches, steps on, and the like.
   b. Encourage her to retell her "walk-talk" later to other members in the family.

Suggested age range: Three to five years

(6) Dramatic Play — Pretend You Are...

Purpose: To encourage the child's use of speech for self-expression and problem solving

Concept: Spoken ideas and feelings help people understand themselves and one another.

Skills

1. Practice with language to express ideas and feelings
2. Observation through listening and watching
3. Use of imagination

Vocabulary

pretend	make believe	role playing
character	stage	

Materials Needed	*Suggested Activities*

Cardboard or paper; scissors; string; crayons

Nurse's cap

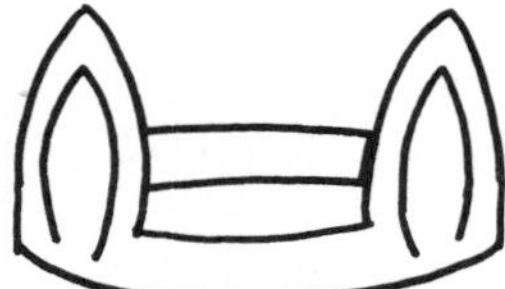

Cat's ears

1. Watch the child at play for clues. For example, if he is using a toy car, suggest that he pretend to be "Daddy" taking the family for a ride.
2. At another time, suggest that the child play-act the role of baby, mother, nurse, kitten, and so on.
3. To help him get started, offer him an object associated with character, such as:
   a. A bottle (for baby)
   b. A handbag (for mother)
4. Make him a nurse's cap or a pair of cat's ears.
5. Encourage him to talk as he plays.
6. If he slows down, join in by addressing him as the character he is play-acting. For example, say, "Baby, let me rock you," or, "Mother, gimme a cookie." Watch his reactions and follow his lead as you play-act.
7. If he needs ideas to continue playing, offer him some ideas ("Pretend you are mad" or "We have to go to the doctor's for a shot").
8. Afterwards, encourage him to talk about what happened and how you both felt in your roles.

9. Switch roles, and play-act again. Discuss what happened, as above.

Puppets (see language development [2])

10. Suggest that the child play-act again, but offer him puppets to use in the play.

Additional or More Difficult Activities

1. May I play?
   a. When the child is involved in dramatic play, ask if you can join in.
   b. Let him assign you a role to play, or make one up yourself.
   c. If he is playing "house" and is the father, address him as "Father."
   d. Follow the theme of the play as he interprets how he wishes it to be.
   e. Talk with him afterwards about what happened and how the characters felt.

Paper, cardboard, flannel, or sturdy fabric scraps; scissors; needle, thread, yarn; paste; crayons, felt pen; popsicle sticks, wooden clothes pins, twigs; box for storage; small stones or rocks

2. Family game
   a. Make flat dolls to represent members of your family (include pets, too).
   b. Paste paper dolls on cardboard for strength.
   c. Make a stage of flat or framed flannel (or turkish toweling) squares about twelve by twelve inches. The lid of a storage box can also serve as a stage if the flannel is pasted inside.
   d. Dress the clothes pin or twig dolls in fabric scraps.
   e. Allow the child to play with the dolls in his own way.
   f. Encourage the child to talk aloud as he plays.
   g. Make additional dolls to represent the child's other relatives, neighbors, friends.

3. Guessing game
   a. Play-act silently something that is familiar to the child (taking a bath). Ask the child to describe what you are doing and to guess what it is.
   b. Turn down the sound on the television and have the child describe and guess what the characters are doing.

4. Dream chant
   a. Make up a tune to accompany the chant: "Dream, dream, sometimes I dream." Sing it to the child, tell him about a dream you had. Encourage him to talk about his dreams.

Cardboard tubes, boxes, box lids; paper; paper brass fastener; yarn about twelve inches long; scissors

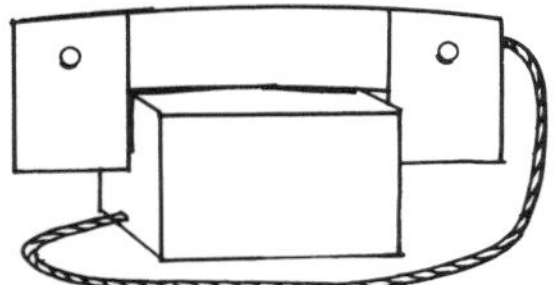

Cardboard phone

5. Telephone calls
   a. Make two telephones from cardboard by attaching mouth and ear pieces with fasteners at each end. Paste yarn (the wire) to box and to ear end.
   b. Call the child on the "phone." Encourage him to talk. If necessary, supply him with ideas ("Can you think of one thing that made you feel good today?").

6. Encourage the child to talk about how he feels when he hears music, sees something beautiful, touches something pleasurable (as velvet), feels drizzle or wind on his face, and so forth.

Suggested age range: Four to five years

(7) Labeling — Name Tag

Purpose: To help the child learn to recognize picture symbols or written labels

Concept: Everything can be described by words which can be spoken, pictured, printed, or written.

Skills

1. Observation
2. Association of picture or printed label to object it describes

Vocabulary

describe	show	picture
symbol	printed	name tag
label	trace	

Materials Needed	*Suggested Activities*
Paper or cardboard; crayon, felt pen, pen, or pencil; sandpaper; scissors; tape  Tracing frame	1. Use manuscript printing (A, B, C, a, b, c, d, e, f, g) for all written labels. *This is important* because the child will be introduced to this kind of printing when she goes to school. 2. Print the child's first name as often as possible on her belongings (Janet; Bobby) and call her attention to it. 3. Make a name tag for her and put it where she can easily see it. If you use large letters cut from sandpaper, she can feel the letters. 4. Cut her name from a piece of cardboard to make a tracing frame for her. 5. If the child seems interested, encourage her to try to copy her name without using the tracing frame (freehand).
	Additional or More Difficult Activities
Construction paper or cardboard; felt pen or crayon; tape  	1. Label cards a. Make labels for objects that the child uses. If you add a picture to the printed word, it will help her recognize the label more easily. b. Prop or tape labels on objects. Talk about these labels with the child. c. When she recognizes a label, take it off the object it represents. Later, give the child the label and ask her to put it on the object it matches.

d. Keep making labels and repeating the above process. Remove some of the labels the child has learned and bring them out at a later time to test whether she still recalls them.

Old magazines, catalogs, newspapers; cardboard; scissors; paste

2. Picture cards
   a. As the child learns a label, suggest that she find a picture of the object. Help her cut it out and paste it on a label card, or on a separate sheet of paper on which you have printed the label.

Paper; thread or yarn

   b. Make a scrapbook and divide it into group sections, labeling each ("Clothing"). Use separate pages for each type ("Shoes"). Encourage the child to find the appropriate pictures.

3. Labels everywhere
   a. Talk with the child about labels wherever you see them: groceries on the shelf (at home or in the supermarket); on television; on traffic signs, store fronts, billboards, trucks, busses, and so forth.

Suggested age range: Two and a half to five years

(8) Finger Activities Finger Games

Purpose: To improve speech

Concept: Ideas can be expressed by words and gestures.

Skills

1. Memory
2. Coordination of words with hand movements
3. Enunciation

Vocabulary (Words used in the games)

Suggested Activities

Building a tower

Silence

Head on hands

Arms in circle

Cuddle

Arms up

1. Say the finger game rhyme and show the child the accompanying finger motions (see below).
2. Encourage the child to learn the words first. Repeat them with him many times.
3. When he knows the words, practice the finger motions with him.
4. If he makes up his own finger motions, use his.
5. Ask the child to teach the games to others in the family, and encourage him to do them often.
6. Try to make up finger games with the child that center round his interests, such as: "I play with my toys" (pantomime the action of building a tower) "without making a noise" (put index finger over your lips to show silence). "I sleep in the night" (fold your hands, lay your cheek on them, and close your eyes) "till the sun is bright" (open your eyes, make a big circle with your arms to represent the sun). "I love my kitty-cat" (cuddle your arms and pat an imaginary cat) "Till she brings a rat" (open your arms and hold up your hands).

Traditional Finger Games

1. One little body
   Two little hands to clap, clap, clap!
   Two little feet go tap, tap, tap!
   Two little hands go thump, thump, thump!
   Two little feet go jump, jump, jump!
   One little body turns around,
   One little body sits quietly down.

Little ball

Bigger ball

Great big ball

2. Here's a ball
   a. Make a little ball with fingers (as shown in accompanying diagram).
   b. Make a larger ball with your fingers.
   c. Make a "great big ball" (with arms) while reciting:
   A little ball, a bigger ball,
   A great big ball I see.
   Now let's count the balls:
   One, two, three (repeat small, big, and bigger balls on this line).

3. Here is a beehive
   Here is a beehive (cup hands together),
   But where are the bees?
   Hidden away where nobody sees.
   Soon they'll come creeping (release fingers one by one)
   Out of the hive.
   One, two, three, four, five.
   Bzzzzzzzzzz.

Mouse

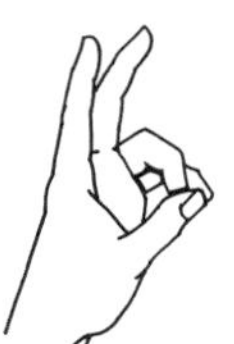

Rabbit

4. Little mousie
   See the little mousie (put fingers on thumb)
   Creeping up the stairs (creep "mouse" up the other arm),
   Looking for a warm nest.
   There, oh, there (let mouse spring into bend of arm)!

5. My rabbit
   My rabbit has two big ears (hold up index and middle fingers for ears)
   And a funny little nose (join other fingers to thumb)
   He likes to nibble carrots (move thumb in "bites")
   And he hops wherever he goes (move entire hand).

6. Making biscuits
   I am making biscuit dough —
   Round and round the beaters go.
   Add some flour from a cup.
   Stir and stir the batter up.
   Roll them; cut them nice and neat.
   Put them on a cookie sheet.
   Bake them; count them: one, two, three.
   Serve them to my friends for tea.

Suggested age range: Three to five years

(9) Characteristics — Let's Discover

Purpose: To become more perceptive of familiar things and to learn about their characteristics

Concept: New information can be learned from the exploration of familiar things.

Skills

1. Observation
2. Exploration
3. Ability to question and to understand how things work
4. Ability to describe

Vocabulary: (Descriptive words of objects investigated)

discover	investigate	different
alike	same	copy
works		

Materials Needed	*Suggested Activities*

1. You and the child carefully study one room at a time. According to her ability to understand, talk about everything, one thing at a time: why it is needed; how it works; what it is made of; how we take care of it; and so forth.
2. Start with the child's possessions. For example, remove the mattress and springs from her bed or crib. Allow the child to examine each. Explain their functions.
3. Turn the bed upside down (if possible). Show the child the frame, how it is held together, and the like. Discuss the different materials used.
4. Proceed at the child's pace.
5. Avoid confusing her by giving her too much information at one time.
6. Encourage the child to ask questions.
7. Ask the child to describe in her own words what she is learning. In this way you will be able to determine how she understands.

8. Suggest that she go through the house to find other objects that are alike. Look at these with her to see if she notices differences and similarities.

Books, magazines, newspapers, catalogs

9. Ask the child to find pictures of similar objects. Talk about them with her.

Additional or More Difficult Activities

Catalogs (which have home appliances) or direction manuals that come with home appliances or a car

1. Find the real one
   a. Show the child a picture of parts of a familiar object (stove, couch). Ask her to find the actual part on the home furniture. Discuss its use, of what it is made.
   b. Ask the child to find a picture of something familiar, then to match the picture to the object. Ask her to tell what is different, what is alike.

Nursery or flower catalog or book on flowers or plants

   c. Repeat the above, using pictures of flowers and plants similar to those in the house or garden, or those in a neighbor's yard.
   d. Encourage the child to find objects in the house which she has seen on television.

Variety of objects, such as: blocks, or wooden ends from a lumber yard; boxes, cartons, cans, or plastic containers; empty spools; thread, film, string, and the like; short twigs or dowel sticks; jar lids; pebbles or stones; scraps of fabric; plastic glue; hammer and nails (optional); storage box

2. Make one like it
   a. Suggest to the child that she make her own copies of what she has investigated (stove).
   b. If she has difficulty doing this, help her in getting started.
   c. Allow her to proceed in her own way.
   d. Encourage her to describe her copy as she makes it.
   e. Accept the child's version, even if it differs from the original. Discuss the differences and similarities.
   f. If the child wishes to keep the finished product, help her put it together so that it will last.
   g. Keep adding to the supply of materials that she can use for building copies of what she sees.

Suggested age range: Two and a half to five years

(10) Learning Trips Start at Home

Purpose: To learn new things and have new experiences

Concept: New information can be learned from unfamiliar things and new experiences.

Skills

1. Observation
2. Exploration
3. Ability to question
4. Ability to describe

Vocabulary (Descriptive words learned on trips)

Materials Needed	*Suggested Activities*
	1. Tell the child that you will "play like" you're taking a trip to find new things, but that you will stay at home.
	2. Find something that will interest him — a sieve, an electric meter box, and so forth.
	3. Follow the same procedure as outlined in language development (9) — "Let's Discover."
	4. During this activity, take him to a storage chest, the attic, the garage, a barn, or some such new place and select articles the child may not have seen before.
	5. Look at family photographs, especially old ones, and take the child on a "trip" to the time before he was born or while he was a baby.
	6. Show the child old books or magazines you may have at hand. Talk about then and now.
	7. Take the child outside and carefully examine everything near the home, such as hedges, walls, plants, trees. Discuss them one by one with the child.
	8. Take a walk near by. Encourage the child to find things he wishes to know more about. Point out anything he misses, such as lines in the concrete, surface of roadway or street, and so on.

Additional or More Difficult Activities

1. City trips
   a. If possible, take the child on many trips, each one to look at something special, such as the airport, a bus depot, a train station, freight yards, the harbor, boatyards, marinas, factories, residential areas.
   b. Each time, discuss what you see.
   c. Encourage the child to ask questions.
   d. Show the child on a map where he has visited. Mark the spots. (Map of city)
   e. Allow the child to look through classified sections of the telephone book to find pictures (in the ads) of things similar to those he has seen. (Phone book; picture books)

2. Country trips
   a. If possible, take the child on many trips, each one to discover something different, such as the woods, a stream, reservoirs, meadows, hills, rocky areas, deserts, farms, dairies, orchards.
   b. Follow the same procedures as for "city trips" above.

3. Park trips
   a. If possible, take the child to nearby parks and to other, more distant parks.
   b. Explore the entire park: recreational areas, lawns, foliage. Talk with the child about everything you see.
   c. Try to prepare a "snack" ahead of time so that you can have a picnic.

4. Library trips
   a. As often as possible, visit the public and other libraries. Find the children's section and allow time for the child to look at books.
   b. Try to visit the library at those times that the librarian has scheduled a story hour.
   c. Borrow books to read to the child at home.

5. Make what you saw (Variety of objects, such as in (9) — "Make One Like It")
   a. Encourage the child to re-create what he saw on all of the trips. Ask him to decribe what he is doing as he works.

Sensory Motor

(1)	Body Awareness	My Body Has . . .
(2)	Throwing and Catching	Fun with Balls
(3)	Strengthening Small Muscles	Twist the Nuts and Bolts
(4)	Spatial Awareness	Position
(5)	Balancing	Balancing Tricks
(6)	Right and Left	Right and Left Directions
(7)	Sense of Hearing	Sound Boxes
(8)	Sense of Smell	Smell Bottles
(9)	Surface Texture	See and Feel Box
(10)	Sequential Order of Sizes	From Littlest to Biggest

Suggested age range: Two and a half to five years

(1) Body Awareness — My Body Has...

Purpose: To learn the names of the parts of the body

Concept: Every part of the body has a name.

Skills
1. Identification
2. Follow directions

Vocabulary

body	head	trunk
arm	leg	forehead
cheek	mouth	chin
ear	neck	chest (and so forth)

Materials Needed	*Suggested Activities*
Large, full-length mirror; beanbag or small ball (see sensory motor [2] — "Beanbag Tricks")	1. Ask the child to stand before the mirror. Show him the different parts of his body, one by one, and help him learn the name of each.
	2. Say, "Your body is from head to toe. It is all of you. We'll play a game. Touch the part I name."
	3. Ask the child to place the beanbag (or ball) on each part as you name it.
	4. Then ask the child to place the beanbag on parts of your body as you name them.
	5. Ask the child to touch one body part to another (wrist to elbow, finger to toe, and so forth).
Large sheet of paper; crayons or felt pen; scissors	6. Ask the child to lie on the paper, which is flat on the floor (or other surface), then trace an outline of his body. Cut this "silhouette" out.
	7. With the child's help, fill in the body parts, talking to him about the parts as you do so.
	8. Make similar body pictures of other family members. Also trace dolls, teddy bears, and the like.

Photographs, magazines, books

9. Show the child pictures of people. Encourage him to point out and identify the different body parts.
10. Discuss the parts of the body as the child watches television.

Additional or More Difficult Activities

1. More about my body
   a. Sing the following song at bath time to the tune of "Here We Go Round the Mulberry Bush":
      This is the way we wash our arms,
      Wash our arms, wash our arms (and so on)
   Tell the child to touch different body parts with wash cloth as you sing them.

Paper, pencil, and crayons

   b. Place the child's hand or foot (or both, one at a time) on a paper and trace the outline. Color in the nails. Identify palms and backs of hands, tops and soles of feet. Ask the child to learn and name these body parts.
   c. Ask the child to close his eyes. Touch parts of his body, asking him to name them as you do. Vary this activity by using a feather, a toothpick, or a piece of cotton.

Paper, crayons

2. What's missing?
   a. Draw a figure on a piece of paper, leaving off a part (such as an arm).
   b. Ask the child to talk about the picture. If he does not notice that an arm is not there, ask him, "What's missing?"

3. Pictures
   a. If the child is capable, ask him to draw a picture of someone. Discuss what he draws.
   b. If he has forgotten certain parts, ask him to look at himself in the mirror, then return to the drawing to see if he can discover what is missing.

Old magazines or catalogs; scissors; paste; cardboard (the heavier, the better)

4. Body puzzles
   a. Find a picture of one person. Cut it out and paste it on the cardboard. Trim the cardboard to the contours of the figure.
   b. Cut the picture into four parts (straightness doesn't matter).
   c. Mix the four pieces and ask the child to see if he can put them together again, naming the body parts as he reconstructs the puzzle.
   d. When the child is able to piece the puzzle together easily, cut these parts into smaller parts. Ask him to reassemble the body puzzle from the smaller parts.
   e. Find a picture of two people standing or sitting adjacent to one another. Make a puzzle and follow the same procedure as above.
   f. As the child learns how to reassemble puzzles, make more difficult ones. Try using pictures of animals, too.

Suggested age range: Three to five years

(2) Throwing and Catching

Fun with Balls

Purpose: To improve tracking and eye-hand coordination

Concepts

1. It is necessary to use our eyes to determine the position of moving or stationary objects.
2. Eyes and hands can be used together for doing certain things.

Skills

1. Ability to use eyes to follow position of stationary or moving objects
2. Ability to use eyes and hands together for accomplishing certain things
3. Follow directions

Vocabulary

follow	watch	aim
roll	catch	throw
bounce	jump	straight line

Materials Needed	*Suggested Activities*
Soft ball, six or eight inches in diameter; or an empty oatmeal box	1. Explain to the child how to follow moving objects with her eyes. 2. Roll a ball (or box) and watch her eyes to determine if she has understood. 3. Ask her to roll the ball. Let her practice rolling it in a straight line. 4. Place an object about three feet from the child and ask her to roll the ball to the object. As she improves, make the distance greater. 5. Now let her practice throwing the ball. 6. Ask her to throw the ball into the air no higher than her head and then catch it with both hands; then one hand; then the other. 7. Gently throw the ball to the child from close range. Encourage her to watch it carefully and try to catch it before it touches her body. 8. As the child improves, throw the ball to her from a greater distance.

9. If the child has learned how to bounce a ball, ask her to bounce it low and pass one leg over it.

Additional or More Difficult Activities

Beanbag; fabric for making beanbag (such as denim); dried beans; needle, strong thread; scissors

1. Beanbag tricks
   a. To make beanbag, cut out two round pieces of fabric about seven inches in diameter. Using a lock stitch, sew edges, leaving a one-inch space into which to put the beans.
   b. Turn stitched fabric inside out and pour the beans in until the bag is filled. Finish sewing the edges closed.
   c. Ask the child to throw the beanbag into the air, catching it first with both hands, then alternate hands.
   d. Show her how to throw the bag in the air, clap hands once, and then catch the bag. Help her learn how to do this.
   e. As she improves, encourage her to throw the bag higher and clap her hands more than once before catching the bag.
   f. Next, show her how to throw the beanbag into the air and turn a complete circle before catching it.

Empty pail, box, or basket

   g. Place the pail (box or basket) about three feet from the child. Tell her to throw the beanbag into it. As she improves, move the pail farther away.

Plastic container with handle; ball (ping pong, or one made of crumpled paper)

2. Catch it!
   a. Cut off the bottom of a large, clean, plastic container. Turn it upside down and give it to the child to use as a scoop.
   b. Gently throw the ping pong ball (paper ball) to her and tell her to catch it with the scoop.
   c. As she improves in this activity, vary how you throw it (from low to high).
   d. Give the child the ball to throw at you for you to catch in the scoop.
   e. Show her how to throw the ball into the air, turn, and then catch the ball in the scoop. Let her try to do this.
   f. Set the scoop on the ground (floor) and ask the child to try to throw the ball into it. As she improves, move the scoop farther away.

Scoop used as "basketball" hoop

Suggested age range: Three to five years

(3) Strengthening Small Muscles

Twist the Nuts and Bolts

Purpose: To coordinate eyes and hands by learning certain skills

Concept: It is necessary to use our eyes to guide what we want our hands to do.

Skills

1. Eye-hand coordination
2. Use of small muscles of wrists and fingers
3. Close observation
4. Eye tracking

Vocabulary

nut	bolt	grasp
crumple	tear	tighten

Materials Needed	*Suggested Activities*
Nuts and bolts, assorted sizes	1. Select largest nut and bolt and show the child how to hold the nut in one hand, the bolt in the other, and then twist the parts. 2. Help him do this himself. 3. When he is able to do this with ease, give him the next-size (smaller) nut and bolt. Ask him to tighten them as he did the larger ones. 4. Ask him to do this with all of the remaining nuts and bolts, making sure they are in matched pairs. 5. Ask him to *un*twist all of the sets, mix them up, match those that go together, and then retwist them together. 6. When he can do all of the sets easily, ask him to try to twist them together with his eyes closed.
	Additional or More Difficult Activities
Wooden or plastic spring-type clothes pins; roofing nails (large heads); flat box or pie tin	1. Clip the clothes pin a. Show the child how to grasp the clothes pin and pick up a nail, then release the nail into the container.

b. Help him learn to do this by himself.
c. Arrange pins in a line, a circle, a square, and the like, and ask him to pick them up and put them on the flat surfaces or in the container in the same arrangement.
d. Suggest that he clip the pins to the edge of the container.

Newspaper

2. Crumpling
a. Give the child half a sheet of newspaper and ask him to crumple it into as small a ball as he is able.
b. Next, ask him to use only one hand to crumple another half sheet (wash newsprint off his hands when this activity is over).

Paper (construction or notebook); paste

3. Tearing
a. Ask the child to tear the paper into small and large bits or shapes (see mathematics [6] — "Geometric Shapes")
b. Suggest that he paste the torn pieces on a sheet of paper (or in his shape booklet).

Waxed paper; lukewarm iron; tape

c. Cut two pieces of waxed paper the same size. Place one on an ironing board (or other suitable surface) and encourage the child to place his torn pieces of paper on it. Then carefully place the other sheet of waxed paper over these, matching edges of both pieces of waxed paper. Press with lukewarm iron. (Finished product can be hung in a window, taped to a refrigerator, or used as a place mat.)

Plastic meat trays (from butcher) or cardboard; hole puncher; old shoelaces, or yarn or string; tape

4. Starting to sew
a. Punch holes in the trays or cardboard one inch apart.
b. Give the child the shoelaces (or yarn or string cut twelve inches long, the ends of which have been tightly taped for ease of handling).
c. Tell the child to sew in and out of the holes.
d. If you give the child several strings, he can sew them in different holes to make a free-form design.

Thick cardboard square; short zipper (used); old shirt front with large buttons; large snaps; scraps of fabric; stapler (or glue)

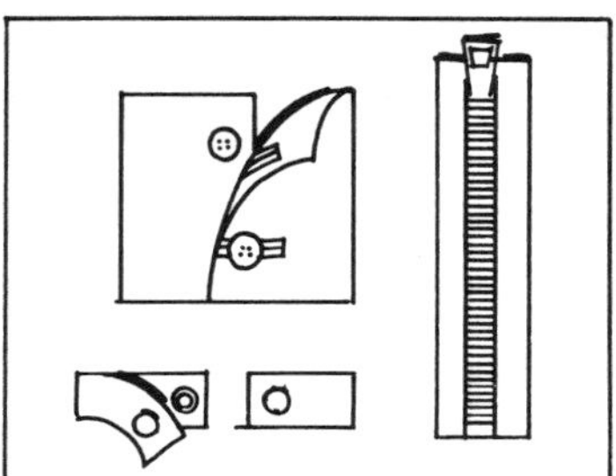

5. Dressing board
a. Sew large snaps on fabric scraps.
b. Staple or glue all items onto the board.
c. Ask the child to practice opening and closing the various items on the board.

Suggested age range: Three to five years

(4) Spatial Awareness Position

Purpose: To develop spatial awareness and an understanding of position in space

Concept: The position of everything in space can be described.

Skills

1. Observation
2. Ability to describe position
3. Ability to follow directions

Vocabulary

over	under	on
above	below	top
bottom	front	back
behind	around	in
out	inside	outside
up	down	near
far	forward	backward
giant	tiny	mirror

Materials Needed	*Suggested Activities*
Small, open, see-through box, or plastic, lattice fruit box; any small object, such as a jar lid	1. Show the child the relationship as you hold the jar lid over, under, and on the box. 2. Ask her to identify the lid's position as you continue to demonstrate, then let her arrange positions of the lid. Encourage her to use the proper words.
Grocery carton, or low table	3. Next, ask her to place herself correctly in relation to the carton, as you call out the positions. 4. When she knows these positions, introduce her to "above," "below," on "top" of, on "bottom" of, following the same steps as above. 5. Gradually add more positions: in front of, behind, around, beside, next to, in, out, inside, outside, up, down.

Flannel board (see language development [6] — "Pretend You Are"); flannel objects; books or magazines

6. Using a flannel board and flannel objects, repeat the steps outlined above.
7. Look at pictures with the child and ask her to point to and describe positions of objects and people in relation to one another.
8. Whenever possible, encourage the child to talk about the positions of objects and people.

Additional or More Difficult Activities

Small objects, such as spool, can, crayon, or spoon

1. Near or far?
   a. Ask the child to sit on the floor. Place some objects near her and some far away, using these words to describe where you are putting them.
   b. Ask the child to touch the "near" objects, then the "far" ones.
   c. Next, ask her to place objects "near" and "far" from you.
   d. Tell her to take one object and place the others — some "near" and some "far" from it.
   e. Place objects near and far from the child. After she has studied their positions for a while, ask her to close her eyes and point in the direction of each object as you name it. Ask her whether it is "near" or "far."
2. Take a giant step
   a. Play this game outside, if possible.
   b. Sing or chant directions to the child, such as: "Take a giant step forward, backward; now take a tiny step up, a giant step down." Vary your directions with other position words.
   c. As the child improves, sing the chant faster.
   d. Ask the child to sing directions to you.
   e. Ask her to play the game, singing her descriptions of what she is doing as she does it.
3. Mirror game
   a. Face the child. Move your arms to different positions (placing them on "top" of head, pointing "down," "up," and so forth).
   b. Ask her to "mirror" (copy, as with reflection in a mirror) what you are doing, and to describe the positions of your hands.
   c. Next, let the child make the movements and describe them, and you "mirror" what she does.

Suggested age range: Three to five years

(5) Balancing

Balancing Tricks

Purpose: To learn how to maintain balance while performing certain skills

Concepts
1. Balance is influenced by where one's weight is.
2. Parts of the body may be moved to correct imbalance.

Skills
1. Concentration
2. Perception
3. Ability to keep self in balance

Vocabulary

balance	lose balance (imbalance)	sideways
forward	backward	tiptoe

Materials Needed	*Suggested Activities*

1. Ask the child to stand on one foot for as long as he can. Count the seconds. See if he can do this for as long as ten seconds without losing his balance.
2. Tell him to try this on the other foot.
3. Ask him to repeat both of the above with his eyes closed.
4. Ask the child to stand on one foot while raising his other leg toward the front, then to the side, then behind him.
5. Ask him to stand on tiptoe on both feet for ten seconds. When he can do this, tell him to shut his eyes and repeat the activity.
6. Next, tell him to stand on his tiptoes with his hands on his hips for as long as he can.
7. Ask him to stand on his toes with his feet close together, then far apart. Count the seconds he can maintain his balance.
8. Suggest that he stand on his toes with his feet far apart and put his arms out to the sides. When he does this, ask him to move his arms in circles while on tiptoe.

9. Encourage the child to practice these balancing tricks as often as possible.

Additional or More Difficult Activities

Length of rope or string (six to ten inches long); line or crack in ground or line of stripe in carpet or floor; edge of sandbox

1. Tightrope walker
   a. Place the rope (string) in a straight line. Show the child how to walk forward, touching heel to toe.
   b. Ask the child to copy what you did.
   c. When he can do this, ask him to walk backwards along the line, heel to toe.
   d. Next, ask him to walk along the line without looking at it or at his feet.
   e. Suggest that he walk to the middle of the line, balance himself on one foot, turn on one foot, and walk backwards (he will end up at opposite end from where he started this activity).
   f. Tell him to walk once more to the middle, stand on one foot (other foot raised backwards), with his arms out. Count the seconds he can maintain balance.
   g. Ask him to walk across the line in a sideward motion ("sideways").
   h. Have him repeat this with his eyes closed.

Any object

   i. Put an object at the center of the line. Ask the child to walk along the line and step over the object without losing his balance.
   j. Suggest that he walk to the middle (object has been removed) and do a trick (putting both arms out and turning, and the like) without losing his balance.

2. Walking in circles
   a. Place the rope (or string) in a circle.
   b. Ask the child to walk along it, heel to toe.
   c. Tell him to walk backwards round the circle.
   d. Suggest that he hop along the rope circle, a few hops with one foot, then with the other.
   e. Tell the child to go half way round the circle by hopping on one foot ten times, then rebalancing himself, and continuing round the full circle.
   f. Encourage the child to test his balance whenever you find an appropriate place, such as a low wall, ramp, broad lower step, or low (safe) cliff.

Suggested age range: Four to five years

(6) Right and Left

Right and Left Directions

Purpose: To learn right and left in relation to own body and right and left directions

Concepts

1. Our bodies are two-sided — right and left.
2. Position can be described according to directions of right and left.

Skills

1. Recognition of right and left sides of own body
2. Recognition of right and left directions
3. Concentration
4. Ability to follow directions

Vocabulary

right
footprint
left
direction

Materials Needed	*Suggested Activities*
Paper; pencil or crayon	1. Explain to the child about the right and left sides of her body. 2. Trace the child's right hand on paper, then trace her left hand. Discuss *right* and *left* as you work. 3. Cut out the tracings and print Right and Left on the proper ones. 4. Ask the child to match her hands to the tracings. 5. Mix the tracings up and tell her to find the correct one for each hand and then to name it. 6. Trace the child's feet and follow the above procedure. 7. When the child can name her hands and feet correctly, ask her to show you where her right arm, leg, knee, eye, and so forth, are; then have her do the same with the left parts of her body. 8. Encourage the child to name *right* and *left* parts of her body as often as possible.

Additional or More Difficult Activities

Cardboard; scissors; colored chalk or charcoal for floor; stick or twig for ground

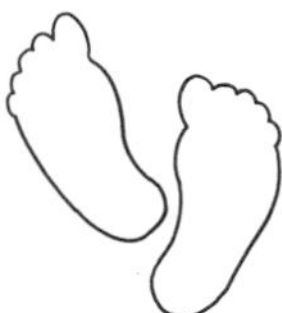

Footprints

1. Footprints
   a. Trace the child's right foot on the cardboard. Print Right on it. Cut it out and turn the cardboard over and print Left on the opposite site.
   b. Make a footprint path on the floor or ground in a circle or a straight line by tracing the cardboard foot in a walking pattern. For example, first the right foot, then the left foot farther ahead.
   c. Ask the child to walk on the footprints, placing her feet correctly. Tell her to say "right" and "left" as she walks.
   d. Next, ask her to repeat this by going backwards.
   e. Vary the activity by asking her to hop with the left foot on the *left* prints but walk with the right foot on the *right* prints.
   f. Call out directions for her to follow: "Step right," "Hop right," "Step left," and so on.
   g. Change the pattern of the footprint path from time to time to make the activity harder.

Handprints and footprints

2. Match and see
   a. Put handprints on a table, footprints on the floor.
   b. Tell the child to put her hand or foot on the appropriate print as you name it: "Left hand," "Left foot," "Right foot," and so on. As the child improves, call out the directions faster.
   c. Ask the child to do the naming for you. Do some of yours wrong, and see if she finds your mistakes.

3. Simon says
   a. Ask the child to listen for what Simon says, such as: "Simon says, 'Touch your right ear,' " or "left cheek," or "left big toe," or "right knee."
   b. Repeat the steps as in "match and see" above.

Small piece of string

4. What's on the right?
   a. Tie the string on the child's right wrist. As she does everything, ask her to tell you when she moves to the right, what she sees on the right.

Picture book or magazine

   b. Look at pictures with the child. Ask her to point to everything on the *right* page, and on the *right* side of the page.

5. What's on the left?
   a. Repeat steps of activity above.

Suggested age range: Three to five years

(7) Sense of Hearing — Sound Boxes

Purpose: To help the child learn to distinguish between the different sounds that he or she hears

Concepts

1. We hear through our ears.
2. The ability to hear is important for many reasons; it helps us talk, protect ourselves, learn to know the differences between sounds, be able to appreciate and duplicate music, and so forth.

Skills

1. Ability to listen attentively
2. Ability to hear differences in sounds (type of sound, volume, pitch, tone, and so forth)
3. Ability to duplicate sounds heard

Vocabulary

hear	sound	high
low	soft	loud

Materials Needed	*Suggested Activities*
Small containers with lids (boxes, food cartons, pill bottles, film boxes); different materials (rice, screws, buttons, paper clips, cotton, pennies, pebbles, twigs, leaves, bottle caps)	1. Show the child three different materials (screw, twigs, and cotton). 2. Place each type of material in a small box (you'll have three boxes). 3. Shake the boxes and ask the child to listen to the sound each box makes. 4. Discuss the different sounds with the child. 5. Encourage the child to experiment with the "sound boxes," and discuss what he hears in them. 6. One by one, introduce additional materials and follow the procedure outlined above. 7. Encourage the child to duplicate the sounds he hears by using his own voice.

Additional or More Difficult Activities

Four to seven identical drinking glasses; spoon; small cream pitcher or large milk pitcher; towel; water

1. Musical glasses
   a. Set up the glasses, pitcher, and water on sink or other place that is safe for water activity.
   b. Start by filling the first glass with a small amount of water, and then striking it gently with the spoon. Ask the child to listen.
   c. Fill a second glass with an equal amount of water, and strike it. Then add a little more water, strike the glass again, and discuss with the child the differences in the sound. Continue increasing the number of glasses and the amounts of water until the set is filled.
   d. Ask the child to experiment by striking the glasses.
   e. If tonal quality is adequate, try playing a familiar tune on the glasses ("Mary had a little lamb, little lamb, little lamb"). Help the child recognize the tune.

2. What do you hear?
   a. Ask the child to cover his ears. Then ask him to listen so that he can name various customary sounds heard in the house (water running from a faucet, the radio, boiling water, snoring, and the like).

3. Listening walk
   a. Take the child for a walk. Encourage him to listen for different sounds (car wheels, overhead planes, the song or chirping of birds, leaves falling from trees, sounds made by people's feet as they walk, voices, the wind).

4. Listening for numbers
   a. Review with the child the names of numerals.
   b. Ask him to listen as you say different words and to clap his hands when he hears you give the name of a numeral:

tree	treat	three	free
shoe	two	chew	moo
hive	live	dive	five
four	poor	floor	snore
run	ton	one	none
hen	pen	ten	men
six	fix	mix	sticks
date	late	eight	freight
pine	nine	sign	fine
seven	heaven	leaven	raven

5. Make a sound
   a. Encourage the child to experiment with the different sounds he can make by: running his fingers through a button box; running his fingernails along the sink, a window pane, his shoe; walking on carpet, a wooden floor, through leaves, and so forth.

Suggested age range: Three to five years

(8) Sense of Smell — Smell Bottles

Purpose: To help the child learn to distinguish between the different odors she smells

Concepts

1. We use our noses to detect different smells (odors)
2. The ability to smell is important for many reasons; it helps us protect ourselves, learn to know the differences between odors, determine the different stages of cooking food; know when something has gone bad (as rancid butter), and so forth.

Skills

1. Ability to use the sense of smell
2. Ability to detect differences in odors

Vocabulary

nose	nostril	odor
sour	sweet	burnt (burned)
rancid	strong	weak

Materials Needed	*Suggested Activities*
Small containers with lids, such as food cartons, pill bottles, film boxes; cotton; different things which have odors (onion powder, pepper, powdered coffee or coffee grounds, chili sauce, alcohol, perfume)	1. Fill four to six containers (separately) with small amounts of different things (pepper, powdered coffee, and so on). If using a liquid, such as alcohol, drop a few drops on a small piece of cotton. 2. Ask the child to smell one thing at a time. Discuss with her the kind of odor each item has. If possible, show her the original thing — such as an onion if you are using onion powder. 3. When she has become familiar with the odors, mix up the containers. Ask her to identify the odor of each. 4. Put lids on the containers for storage. 5. Reintroduce these containers at a later time to see if the child can still identify the odors correctly.

Additional or More Difficult Activities

1. Different smells
   a. Whenever an odor is noticeable, ask the child if she can identify it. Discuss with her the differences among odors.

2. Smelling walk
   a. Take the child on a "smelling walk." Encourage her to be on the alert to notice and describe the different odors she smells.

Different cooking odors

3. What's cooking?
   a. Call the child's attention to the odors which come from the kitchen during meal preparation.
   b. Ask her to tell you what she thinks is cooking and why she believes it is a particular food.

Match; burnt toast or food; burnt piece of wool or other fabric

4. Warning game
   a. To acquaint the child with odors that might mean trouble, allow her to smell objects that have been (deliberately or accidentally) burned (match, toast, wool, and the like).
   b. Have similar unburned objects available for her to use as comparison. Ask her to smell them carefully.
   c. Mix burned and unburned objects, cover her eyes so that she cannot peek, and ask her to smell one object at a time and tell you whether it has been burned.

Various small objects (wool sock, cup, paper towel, flower, leather purse)

5. Wet or dry smells
   a. Ask the child to smell the objects you have prepared from the list at left.
   b. Moisten a similar set of objects until they are wet enough to change odor.
   c. Allow the child to smell the moistened items.
   d. Mix the wet and the dry items, cover her eyes so that she cannot peek, and ask her to smell one item at a time. Ask her to tell you whether the item is wet or dry.

Suggested age range: Two and a half to five years

(9) Surface Texture See and Feel Box

Purpose: To learn to distinguish between different textures by sight and feel

Concepts

1. The surface of everything we see can be described as to texture.
2. There are many different kinds of textures.

Skills

1. Ability to use senses of sight and touch
2. Ability to distinguish between different textures

Vocabulary

see	feel	smooth
rough	soft	hard
hot	cold	

Materials Needed	*Suggested Activities*

Box, medium or large; old sock; various items (stones, buttons, jar lids, clothes pins, brush, steel wool, nail file, quarter, pieces of paper, foil, rope, plastic, sandpaper, velvet, denim, corduroy, voile)

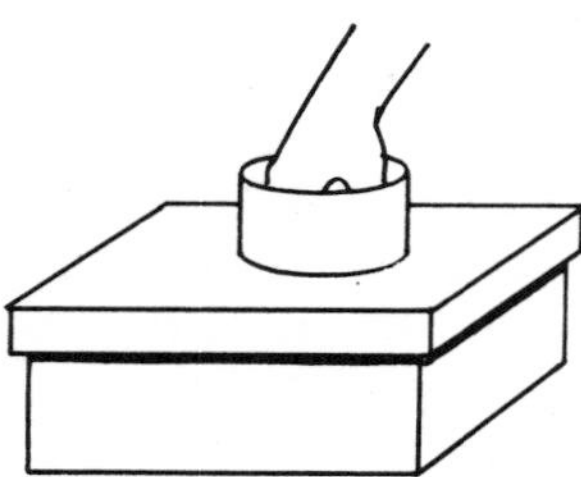

Feel box

1. In the lid of the box, cut a hole large enough for the child to get his hand through.
2. Cut the foot off an old sock and attach the sock firmly round the edge of the hole. (See below, following listings at the left.)
3. Place many items in the box.
4. Ask the child to take an item from the box. Discuss its texture with him. Ask him to feel its surface and describe it.
5. Repeat this with every item until he is familiar with each one.
6. Put the items back into the box and mix them. Put the lid on the box.
7. Ask the child to put his hand through the sock hole, feel one object, and try to describe what it is before taking it out and looking at it.
8. As the child completes the identification of each item, have him place it in a pile with the other items with similar textures (all smooth in one stack, all rough in another).

Old magazines or newspapers

9. Cut out pictures of items whose surface textures are similar to those in the box.

10. Ask the child to sort the pictures according to texture, and and then to place them in the appropriate stacks of sorted objects.

Additional or More Difficult Activities

Crayons (the thicker, the better); paper; items with varying textures (smooth plate, corrugated plastic trays, coins, cane chair seat)

1. Crayon rubbing
   a. Select a smooth and a rough object. Ask the child to look at them, feel them, and then describe them as either smooth or rough.
   b. Put paper over a smooth object. Ask the child to rub crayon over it. Repeat the same procedure with a rough object. Discuss the two rubbings with him.
   c. Locate other things in the house which the child can "crayon rub."
   d. Find interesting things outside for the child to crayon or chalk rub.
   e. Ask the child to select some of his favorite rubbings and hang them low enough on the refrigerator, a door, or a wall so that he can see them. Encourage him to discuss their different textures with you.

Small pieces of paper, or string, yarn, or ribbon

2. Find everything smooth or rough
   a. Suggest to the child that he go through the house and look for all objects which are smooth. As he locates each, tell him to mark it with a small piece of paper or the string or yarn he is carrying.
   b. Later, accompany him through the rooms to see and discuss with him the smooth items he has found.
   c. Repeat this activity, asking him to find rough objects.

Paper, paper bags, or wrapping paper; needle and thick thread or wool; hole puncher (optional); paste or glue; different textured items (fabric, wallpaper samples, yarn, string, rope, various samples of paper, toothpicks, straws, elastic bands)

3. Texture book
   a. Make a notebook in which the child can paste lightweight samples of various textured materials.
   b. Ask him to sort these materials.
   c. Help him paste them into the book, in the groups into which he sorted them.
   d. Ask him to describe the characteristics of each group. Print his discription under each one.

Suggested age range: Three to five years

(10) Sequential Order of Sizes

From Littlest to Biggest

Purpose: To learn how to put things in correct sequential order

Concept: Things can be placed in order and described according to size.

Skills

1. Visual discrimination
2. Hand-eye coordination
3. Ability to place objects in sequential order
4. Small muscle manipulation

Vocabulary

size	little	big
bigger	even bigger	biggest
littler	even littler	littlest
small	large	

Materials Needed	*Suggested Activities*
	1. Talk to the child about *little* and *big* objects.
	2. Ask her to show you "little" objects and "big" objects in the house.
Picture books and magazines	3. Show the child pictures and ask her to point to little and big objects.
Any articles (cans, jar lids, socks of different sizes)	4. Now show her three similar items of different sizes (teaspoon, soup spoon, tablespoon). Discuss them with her: "This is *little*. This is *bigger*. This is *even bigger*."
	5. Mix up the items and ask the child to put them in sequential order.
	6. Give the child other similar objects of different sizes. Ask her to put them in order from littlest to biggest.
	7. Mix up both sets of items. Tell the child, "Find the *biggest* spoon. Put it where it belongs. Now find the *littlest* can. Put it where it belongs." Continue this until all of the six items are in order.

8. When the child can do the last game easily, add a fourth object to the set. Discuss with the child its order and how to describe it; for example, if you select a lid smaller than the others, tell her, "This is the *littlest* lid. Find a *bigger* one which belongs next to it. Put an *even bigger* one next to it. Find the *biggest* of all the lids."

Additional or More Difficult Activities

Four different sizes of empty containers with lids; four different sizes of items; pencil; scissors (or exacto knife)

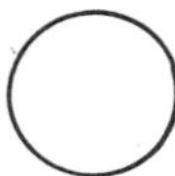
Lid

Pebble

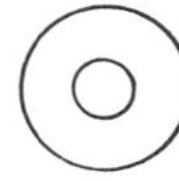
Traced size

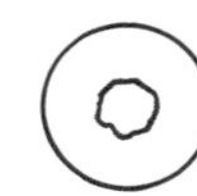
Cut out

1. Push through
   a. Match items to containers. Trace the size of the item on the lid. Carefully cut the lid so that the object can be pushed through it. (See diagram in opposite column.)
   b. Give the child the mixed containers with the lids on and give her matching items. Ask her to put each set in correct order, then push the items through the opening in the lid.
   c. When the child can do this, ask her if she can match the sets at random.

Four different sizes of empty food cartons with lids; four different sizes of items (pebbles, buttons, and the like)

2. Hide the pebbles (buttons)
   a. Show the child the cartons, the lids, and the pebbles (buttons). Ask her to put them in order from littlest to biggest.
   b. Ask the child to cover her eyes. Put everything in the wrong order (pebbles in cartons, lids on cartons, cartons in a line).
   c. Tell the child to look, and ask her to put everything in correct order according to size.

One cup flour; one-half cup salt; cold water; one tablespoonful cooking oil (optional); plastic knife or popsicle stick (optional); four sets of different-size items (as above activity)

3. Play dough bits
   a. With the child's help, make play dough by mixing the dry ingredients and gradually adding a few drops of water until dough can be kneaded without sticking to fingers.
   b. Ask the child to cut or tear off four *little* pieces of dough, then four *even bigger* pieces, then four that will be the *biggest*.
   c. Ask her to arrange all of the dough pieces in correct order; then the different-size items in order.
   d. Tell her to cover her eyes. Mix the dough bits and items.
   e. Ask the child to unscramble them and put them in their correct order.

Old magazines and catalogs; scissors

4. Four sizes of pictures
   a. Suggest that the child find pictures of similar items of different sizes.
   b. Help her cut them out.
   c. Mix up the pictures.
   d. Ask the child to put them in their correct order for size.

Science

(1)	Properties	Floating Objects
(2)	Magnetic Attraction	Magic Magnet
(3)	Balance	Let's Balance
(4)	Changing of Seasons	All-Year Tree
(5)	Cooking	See, Feel, and Taste What Happens
(6)	Tools	Tool Hunt
(7)	Growth	What Do We Need to Grow?
(8)	Water	Wonderful Water
(9)	Air	Our Breath
(10)	Temperature	Hot and Cold

Suggested age range: Three to five years

(1) Properties — Floating Objects

Purpose: To determine what floats

Concept: Some things float because of the material of which they are made (such as a cork); others float because of the way they are made (such as a boat).

Skills
1. Observation
2. Language
3. Experimentation
4. Speculation

Vocabulary

float	sink	waterlogged
light	heavy	wood
plastic	cork	saturate
experiment		

Materials Needed	*Suggested Activities*
Container with water (small bowl, wash basin, tub, sink, puddle)	1. Using one object which floats and one which sinks, explain the reasons for this as you demonstrate to the child what happens when they are placed in a container of water. 2. Give the child more objects with which she can experiment.
Household items (corks, bottle tops, soaps of different components, sticks, small toys, sponge, pebbles, plastic items)	3. Suggest that the child find other objects which she thinks will float or sink. 4. Discuss with the child what happens with each item she puts on the water. 5. Encourage the child to ask questions and speculate about various familiar objects which are too large for experimentation, such as a plastic ball or table. 6. Ask the child to point to pictures of objects in books, magazines, newspapers, on television, on billboards, at stores, and elsewhere. Let her tell whether she thinks these objects would float or sink.

Additional or More Difficult Activities

Supersaturated piece of wood which the child has seen float before

1. Waterlogged
   a. Ask the child to experiment to see if this piece of wood will still float.
   b. Encourage her to question and speculate as to why the piece of wood now sinks (heavy with water).
   c. Give the child another piece of wood, show her how to saturate it, and then ask her to experiment again.

Plastic meat tray; several small items that will weight the tray

2. Pile on
   a. Ask the child to "float" the tray.
   b. Next, ask her to pile the items on the tray, one by one.
   c. Discuss with her why the tray eventually sinks.

Any body of water where the child and adult can swim

3. People float
   a. Demonstrate to the child how to float.
   b. Help the child try to learn to float by herself.
   c. Discuss with her why her body can remain on the surface of the water when she is in the floating position (air in the lungs).

Suggested age range: Three to five years

(2) Magnetic Attraction Magic Magnet

Purpose: To determine which objects a magnet attracts and which it does not

Concepts

1. Magnets have a force which attracts
2. Magnets attract only those objects made of iron, steel, or alloy.

Skills

1. Ability to experiment
2. Growing understanding of which objects a magnet will attract and which they will not
3. Manual dexterity

Vocabulary

magnet	force	attract
iron	steel	alloy
filings		

Materials Needed	*Suggested Activities*
Magnet, either one purchased in a hardware store or the kind used in potholders; many small items (nail, screw, chalk, paper clip, penny, crayon, yarn, paper, pebble, spool); two boxes	1. Show the magnet to the child and explain how it works. 2. Demonstrate its pull by using several items that it will attract (nail, screw, paper clip). 3. Allow the child to experiment by himself. 4. Introduce several items that the magnet will not attract (yarn, paper, spool). Discuss with the child the differences between the two sets of items. 5. Allow the child to experiment. 6. Add more items, mix them up, and suggest that the child use the magnet. Place the items that the magnet attracts in one box and those that it does not in the other. 7. Encourage the child to explain what is happening each time he uses the magnet.

Additional or More Difficult Activities

1. Try the magnet everywhere
   a. Suggest that the child use the magnet on his clothes to see if anything is attracted.
   b. Ask him to walk about the room, seeing if anything responds to the magnetic attraction.

Lady's handbag and its contents; two empty food cartons; heavy yarn or string; hole puncher; felt pen or crayon

2. Yes and no
   a. Spill the contents of the handbag on the floor. Suggest that the child use the magnet on them and then add these items to the proper box (putting those that were not attracted in the second box).
   b. Punch a hole on either side of each carton.
   c. String heavy yarn or string through and fasten to make a handle. Print "No" on one carton and "Yes" on the other.
   d. Give the child the carton, explaining that he put items that the magnet attracts in "Yes" and those it does not in "No."
   e. Suggest that he walk about the room collecting "Yes" and "No" objects in his cartons.

Thin, easily breakable string

3. Magnet necklace
   a. Attach a small magnet to the thin string.
   b. Tie it round the child's neck so that the magnet hangs down to his waist.
   c. Suggest that he go about the house collecting other "Yes" and "No" items in his cartons.

Dirt or sandpile; small box or paper plate; iron filings or small metallic objects (such as hooks and eyes, snaps, paper clips); plastic wrap (sandwich type); tissue paper

4. Watch the iron filings
   a. Take the child outdoors to a sandpile in which you've hidden small metallic items.
   b. Help him run the magnet through the sand or dirt to collect the metallic items (iron filings, paper clips, snaps, and so forth).
   c. Have him put these items in the box or paper plate.
   d. Tell him to run the magnet on the underneath surface of the box or plate and watch what happens.
   e. Cover the plate (box) with plastic wrap so that he can transport it. It then becomes a simple activity that can be re-used.

Suggested age range: Three and a half to five years

(3) Balance

Let's Balance

Purpose: To compare objects for weight and to learn how to balance them

Concepts

1. Two objects or two sets of objects can be balanced according to their weights.
2. Size and weight are not necessarily related.

Skills

1. Ability to compare weights of objects by holding them
2. Ability to use scale to balance objects

Vocabulary

balance	scale	heavy
light	equal	unequal
different	same	alike
weigh	size	weight

Materials Needed	*Suggested Activities*

Two matching boxes (cereal boxes or cottage cheese or milk cartons); wire coat hanger; string or yarn; hole puncher; many small items for balancing (spools of thread, jar lids, pebbles or stones, toys, rolled up socks, bars of soap)

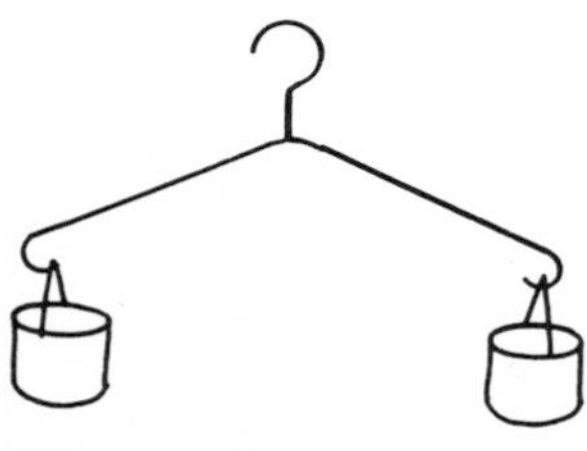

Scale

1. Make a balance scale by punching holes near the top edges of the cartons. Attach three strands of string (at least six inches long) in each hole, then tie the strings together (see illustration in opposite column). Remove the cross bar from the hanger, bend the ends into circles, and attach a carton to each. Suspend the "scale" from a chair or door knob.
2. Show the child how to compare two objects by holding them in your hands. Ask her to try the same thing several times until she seems to understand.
3. Explain what the scale is. Demonstrate how to use it by balancing several sets of objects.
4. Encourage the child to experiment in the use of the scale. Discuss with her what is happening.
5. Suggest that after each set of objects is balanced on the scale, the child place items in separate piles, one heavy and one light (in weight).

Additional or More Difficult Activities

1. Heavy and light
   a. Suggest to the child that she go through the house to collect more objects which she can then compare on the scale.
   b. Help the child sort all of the objects into heavy and light piles. Ask her to use the scale to compare the weights of the separate objects in the light pile. For example, suggest that she compare them to find out if they are equal in weight, or if one is lighter or heavier than the other.
   c. Ask the child to do the same with items from the heavy pile.
   d. Give her one heavy object and ask her to find out how many light objects must be put on the scale to balance the heavy one.

Large wooden plank, or tree limb at least three feet long; heavy wooden box or weighted grocery carton, or flat rock at least one foot high

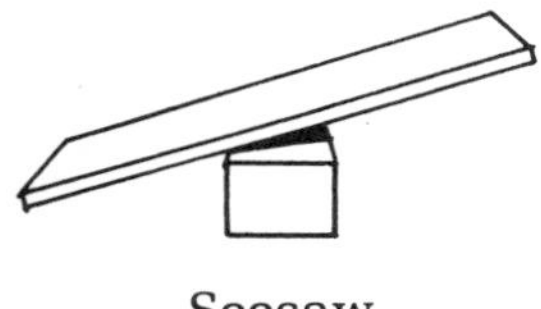

Seesaw

2. Who is heavier?
   a. Make a seesaw (teeter-totter) by placing the center of the plank across a box (see illustration).
   b. Ask the child to sit on one end. Ask another child to sit on the other end (to find out which child is heavier), or place heavy objects on the other end until a balance is reached.
   c. Help the child secure a fairly heavy object, such as a telephone book or several bricks, to one end of the seesaw. Next, ask her to find other objects to use until she makes the seesaw balance.

3. Scales
   a. Try to find a scale that is balanced by weights (such as in in a doctor's office, at a freight station) and weigh the child and yourself (or fairly heavy objects), demonstrating how such a scale is used.
   b. At the supermarket, point out to the child the different kinds of scales that are used (meat weighed in the butcher shop pushes down on the scale; vegetables in the produce section pull down on the scale).

Suggested age range: Two and a half to five years

(4) Changing of Seasons — All-Year Tree

Purpose: To understand the seasonal changes that take place in trees

Concepts

1. Changes occur in nature in each of the four seasons.
2. Seasonal changes are different in different parts of the country and the world.

Skills

1. Observation
2. Ability to notice changes in trees

Vocabulary

seasons	spring	summer
fall (autumn)	winter	frost
rain	snow	sunshine

Materials Needed	*Suggested Activities*

Heavy paper or cardboard, colored construction or tissue paper; scissors; paste or glue; small box for storing tree parts; tape (any kind); cotton or scraps of white fabric

All-Year Tree

1. Cut out a large tree trunk, with branches, from the heavy paper. Glue or tape it to the wall, a door, or refrigerator. Using colored paper, cut out green, yellow, red, and tan leaves; pink, white, yellow, or red buds and blossoms.
2. From cotton, paper, or fabric, make snow for putting on the branches and the ground.
3. Discuss with the child the different seasons of the year and what happens to trees at each season. Suggest that he look outside to see how trees appear at the present time.
4. Show the child the different things you cut out to put on the tree. Ask him first to decorate the All-Year Tree to make it look like the real trees outside. Discuss with him the reasons why trees appear as they do at this time of year (season).
5. Suggest to the child that he decorate the All-Year Tree for each of the other three seasons. Talk with him about each season as he does this.

Additional or More Difficult Activities

Books with pictures of scenery

1. Pictures of the seasons
   a. Look through pictures in books with the child. Suggest that he search for nature pictures, particularly of trees. Ask him to try to figure out which season of the year each picture shows.
   b. Make a scrapbook (see mathematics [5] — "Finding Things That Go Together"). Divide it into four sections, one for each season.

Old magazines; paper or cut-up paper bags; scissors; paste or glue; yarn or string; hole puncher; tape (optional)

   c. Help the child cut out nature pictures from old magazines. (Those which can be used for decorating the All-Year Tree can be mounted on paper to make it easier for him to attach them to the tree.)
   d. Suggest that he paste the other pictures in the scrapbook in the appropriate sections.

Waxed paper; lukewarm iron; hole puncher; string

2. Nature walk
   a. Try to give the child the correct names of plants, leaves, and so forth.
   b. Encourage him to collect fallen leaves, buds, or blossoms. Explain that he cannot pick them off someone else's trees because they are still growing and it is harmful to the trees to remove them before they are ready to fall by themselves.
   c. Some of the fallen leaves, buds, or blossoms can be preserved by putting them between two pieces of waxed paper, which you can press to seal shut. Afterwards, individual leaves can be cut out and pasted in the scrapbook, or a hole can be punched at the top of each (waxed paper enfolded) item and a small piece of string inserted for hanging on the All-Year Tree.
   d. Encourage the child to keep his collections in a box with other things for his All-Year Tree.

Suggested age range: Two and a half to five years

(5) Cooking

See, Feel, and Taste What Happens

Purpose: To understand changes that occur in food when it is cooked

Concept: Raw food undergoes change when it is cooked.

Skills

1. Observation
2. Ability to note and compare changes in appearance, texture, consistency, and taste in food as it is cooked

Vocabulary

raw	cooked	soft
hard	crunchy	watery
solid	peel	skin
boil	fry	scramble
bake	dough	

Materials Needed	*Suggested Activities*
Raw fruit or vegetables (such as an apple or a carrot); cooking utensils; stove	1. Ask the child to eat a piece of fruit or vegetable that she is accustomed to eating raw. 2. Discuss with her its appearance, texture, and taste. 3. Prepare similar food for cooking. Explain what you are doing (peeling, cutting into bits, scraping, coring, tearing). 4. As food is being cooked, let the child feel its consistency with a fork from time to time. Discuss the amount of time it takes for different foods to soften. 5. Serve cooked food to the child. Encourage her to talk about the changes she noted between its raw and cooked stages. 6. Whenever possible, allow the child to help in preparing and cooking the food.

Additional or More Difficult Activities

Assorted vegetables (carrots, potato, celery, parsnip, turnip, onion) made into a soup (recipe: cut vegetables to bite size; cover with water in a pot; season); seasoning; cooking utensils; stove; salad bowl

1. Two-part meal
   a. With the child's help, prepare the vegetables for cooking and for salad (see recipes). Explain why the salad vegetables are sliced into thinner, smaller pieces.
   b. Cook the soup; at the same time, let the child be mixing the raw vegetables in a salad bowl.
   c. Eat the prepared foods. Discuss their differences, and the reasons for these differences.

Recipe for eggnog milkshake: one egg, well beaten; one glass of milk; one tablespoon sugar; one-fourth teaspoon vanilla extract; combine, stir, or shake

2. Magic egg
   a. Show the child the raw egg before you beat it and put it in the eggnog milkshake. Discuss what happens to an egg's consistency when it is beaten.
   b. Let the child drink some of the eggnog.
   c. Allow her to help in beating another egg. Add a little milk or water to it.

Frying pan; butter, oleo, or other grease; salt and pepper

   d. Heat grease in a pan, put in the beaten egg. Ask the child to watch as the consistency and appearance of the egg change as it cooks. Stir occasionally.
   e. Ask the child to eat a bit of the scrambled egg and compare it with the raw eggnog.

Small cooking pot; two eggs

   f. Let the child watch as you place two eggs in a small pot of water. After the water starts to boil, explain to the child that one egg will cook for three minutes and the other for eight minutes.
   g. Allow the child to eat some of each egg after it is cooked and the shell taken off. Discuss with her the differences in the eggs.

Prepare biscuit dough of two cups flour; four teaspoons baking powder; three-fourths cup of milk or water; two and half tablespoons of shortening; one teaspoon salt; pan or cookie sheet (sift dry ingredients; mix shortening in with fork; drop by tablespoon onto greased pan; bake at 350° for ten to twelve minutes

3. Baking's fun
   a. Allow the child to help you prepare the dough.
   b. Give her a taste of the raw dough.
   c. Mix and bake the biscuits, discussing again with her all that you did to get the food ready.
   d. After the child has eaten a baked biscuit, talk to her about the differences between the raw dough and the cooked biscuit.

4. Assistant chef
   a. As often as possible, encourage the child to watch and help with the preparation of food.
   b. Always encourage her to talk about what happens to food between its raw and its cooked stages.

Suggested age range: Three to five years

(6) Tools

Tool Hunt

Purpose: To understand how tools and utensils help us in many ways

Concept: Tools and utensils can make everything we do easier.

Skills

1. Observation
2. Experimentation

Vocabulary

tools	utensils	names of the many tools demonstrated

Materials Needed	*Suggested Activities*
Child's fork, spoon, knife	1. Explain to the child how tools and utensils help us.
	2. Go through the house on a "tool hunt," starting with the child's fork, spoon, and knife. Talk with him about their usefulness.
Kitchen utensils	3. In the kitchen, show the child how each utensil is used — what it does. Allow the child to experiment with each one: paring knife (watch out for sharp edge), potato scraper, egg beater, jar lid opener, rolling pin, flour sifter, soup ladle, and so on.
Grooming articles	4. Ask the child to find things we use to keep ourselves neat: brush, comb, clothes brush, nail brush or file, toothbrush, and so on.
Needles, thimble, darning egg, scissors	5. Explain how sewing tools make it simpler for us to sew and mend.
Telephone book, catalogs, newspapers, or magazines	6. Suggest to the child that he go through the magazine, catalog, or phone book (yellow pages) to find pictures of the tools and utensils he has already found in the house.

	Additional or More Difficult Activities
Hammer, screw driver, saw, file, and the like; nails; wood scraps	1. Tool chest a. Show the child the tools in a tool chest, demonstrating how each tool is used. b. Allow him to experiment with the tools, under your supervision.
Garden tools	2. Gardening is fun a. Find a spot in the yard or garden where the child can dig. b. Allow him to experiment with the garden tools that he can easily handle: rake, spade (shovel), watering can, hoe, or hose.
	3. Car tools a. Take the child to a nearby gas station. b. Ask the attendant or mechanic to show the child some of the tools he uses to work on cars, wash and polish cars, change tires, and so forth. Ask him to explain the tools to the child as he shows them.
	4. Painter's tools a. Visit a paint store. b. Show the child the various tools used by the painter: sandpaper, brushes, pails, ladders, spray guns, and so on.
	5. Hardware store a. Visit a hardware store. b. Look for tools that are used in the home or yard: wrenches, pulleys, plumbers' snakes, levers, and so on. Explain to the child how they are used.
Paper; scissors; paste; felt pen or crayon; old magazines, catalogs, or newspapers	6. Tool scrapbook a. Make a scrapbook. b. Look through the catalog (magazine, or newspaper) with the child and ask him to find pictures of the tools he knows about. Help him cut them out and paste them in a scrapbook. c. Divide the scrapbook into sections and label them "House Tools," "Garden Tools," "Car Tools," and so on.

Suggested age range: Two and a half to five years

(7) Growth

What Do We Need to Grow?

Purpose: To understand the process of growth in living things

Concepts

1. Living things continue to grow until they are mature, or ripe.
2. Growth depends upon certain conditions and care.

Skills

1. Observation
2. Ability to describe

Vocabulary

grow	healthy	sprout
root	seed	muscles
strong	weak	

Materials Needed	*Suggested Activities*
	1. Discuss what babies need to grow: food, sleep, shelter, cleanliness.
Baby photographs of the child; any clothes she has outgrown	2. Show the child her baby pictures, her outgrown clothing. Discuss with her changes that have occurred in her growth.
	3. Ask the child to think of all the things she can do which babies cannot do.
	4. Discuss with her the reasons why she can do so much more. For example, she can walk, her muscles are stronger, she is taller, and so forth.
	5. Talk about her continuing growth and what is done to help her grow strong and remain healthy; for example, the food she eats, the hours she sleeps, the clothes she wears to protect her from the cold, and the like.
	6. Explain why grown-ups stop growing (except for weight).
Pictures on food boxes, cans, or in ads; catalogs (food, clothing, household furnishings)	7. Look at pictures of food and ask the child to talk about what children need to grow.
	8. Look at pictures of clothing and household furnishings (beds, tables, dishes) and discuss with her why we need these things to help us grow.
	Additional or More Difficult Activities
	1. Quick growers
	a. Ask the child to watch as you prepare some "quick growers" (see lists in opposite column as they are described). Whenever possible, allow her to help you.

b. Discuss what you are doing and the plants' need for water and light.
c. Each day, look at the plants with the child. Encourage her to note changes (such as how a plant will follow light when you swivel the holder a bit each day).
d. Teach her to add more water when needed.

Carrots

Two carrots, one at least four inches long; knife; shallow bowl; string

Water
Carrot
Hanging carrot

a. Slice half an inch off the top (leaf end) of a carrot. Put it in a bowl, with water, cut side down. As water evaporates, add more. Fernlike sprouts should start within two to three days.
b. Cut two inches off bottom of another carrot. Scoop out the inside. Punch two holes in the sides at the top; put the string through the holes. Fill the hollow with water. Hang near light. Be sure to check the water frequently.

Sweet Potato

Sweet potato; soup plate or aluminum loaf tin, or a low bowl

a. Slice lengthwise and put both halves in a container of water near a sunny window. Within ten days sprouts will appear.
b. Keep watered. Plant will continue to grow and will last many months.

Onion

Onion; glass jar

a. Squeeze an onion into a glass jar with sprout end up. Growth will start soon.

Dried Beans

Dried beans; saucer; cotton or paper toweling

a. Soak overnight in water.
b. Put in a saucer between two layers of wet cotton or paper toweling. Keep wet. Growth will start in a day or two.

Citrus Seeds

Orange or grapefruit seeds; dirt or sand; small container

a. Place an orange seed (or other citrus fruit) in dirt. Several seeds can be used if they are spaced a little.
b. Water the same as for any house plant. In about a week, a sprout will appear.

Pumpkin Seeds

Dried lentils or squash or pumpkin seeds; dirt or sand; small container

a. Plant the seeds of a pumpkin or squash (or any other gourd or melon) in a small container that has been filled with dirt.
b. Water as you would a house plant. Growth will start in several days.

Ivy

Ivy, indoor or outdoor variety (philodendron or other house plants can be used); transparent glass or jar; planting soil; small container

Diagonal cut

a. Take "slip" from "mother" plant by breaking or cutting below any "crotch" in the larger plant (see diagram in opposite column). If "slip" is cut, be sure to cut on diagonal.
b. Place new start in a jar of water for a few days, or until roots appear.
c. New plant can now be transferred to container of soil that has been wet down well.

Suggested age range: Three to five years

(8) Water Wonderful Water

Purpose: To learn about water, its many uses, how it changes, and its sources

Concepts
1. Water is necessary to sustain life.
2. Water takes on different forms under different conditions.
3. Water comes from many sources.

Skills
1. Observation
2. Experimentation

Vocabulary

rain	hail	sleet
snow	melt	thaw
steam	moisture	temperature
evaporate	dew	fog

Materials Needed	*Suggested Activities*
	1. Talk to the child about the many uses we have for water.
	2. Help him keep count of the times he uses water each day: wash face in morning; flush toilet; wash hands before meals; brush teeth after meals; mother uses in cooking; mother uses in washing dishes, clothes; used in play for water paints; wash doll clothes; water plants and gardens; drink water; ice cubes to cool drinks; bath; wash hair.
	3. Explain how we get water for home use (through pipes from a reservoir, from a spring or a well).
	4. Talk to the child about where water comes from: wells, springs, streams, lakes.
	5. Discuss how fog, rain, hail, sleet, snow, and ice are also sources of water which feed the streams, lakes, and so forth.
Empty pail (bucket)	6. Plan to catch water in a pail during the next storm. At room temperature, this water is excellent for watering plants or rinsing the hair.

Additional or More Difficult Activities

Kettle; stove; cup

1. Making steam
   a. Put a kettle of water on the stove and turn on the burner. Let the child see the steam coming from the spout of the kettle and explain that it is very hot.
   b. Hold a cup near the steam, then let the child see the moisture left in the cup. Let him feel its warmth (after it has cooled a bit).
   c. Call the child's attention to the steam while you cook. Show him how it rises from pots and from hot food, and how it collects on lids of pots.
   d. Show him steam from the hot water faucet in sink, tub, or shower.
   e. Explain how moisture in our breath makes steam on a frosty morning.
   f. Explain that fog and mist are steam that is formed when cold rain touches the warmer ground.
   g. Show the child steam that forms on the inside of car windows on cold days when the car is warmer than the air outside the car.

Ice cube, snow, or ice

2. Water from ice
   a. Explain to the child that ice melts in warmer temperatures.
   b. Take an ice cube or the frost from inside the freezer or refrigerator, or snow or ice from outside, and leave it at room temperature.
   c. Check on a clock to see how long it takes for different-size pieces to melt.

   Water glass or cup

   d. Allow the child to experiment to find out how many melted ice cubes it takes to fill a tumbler or cup.
   e. Keep the melted water from the ice for watering house plants.

3. Evaporation
   a. Explain that water (or any liquid) will evaporate when moisture is dried out of it by the air, especially warm air, or by the sun.
   b. Point out that this evaporated moisture forms clouds which later returns the water to the ground in the form of rain or snow.

   Saucer

   c. Leave a small amount of water in a saucer. Check it with the child several times each day to note how it evaporates.

   Inexpensive housepainter's brush; pail or large can to hold water

   d. Let the child water-paint outside on a sunny day. Ask him to watch how quickly his water-paint brush strokes evaporate from the cement, stone, or wooden surface.

4. Dew
   a. Take the child outside early in the morning to see the dew.
   b. As the sun comes out and warms the air, ask the child to see how quickly the dew disappears.

Suggested age range: Three to five years

(9) Air

Our Breath

Purpose: To teach the effect of air

Concepts

1. Air is invisible. It is recognized by its effect on things.
2. Air is necessary for life.
3. Air has force; it can move things.
4. Air occupies space.

Skills

1. Observation
2. Experimentation

Vocabulary

air	breath	lung
blow	inflate	power
cooling	lightning	float
weight	invisible	occupy

Materials Needed	*Suggested Activities*
	1. Show the child how to take a deep breath and expell air from the lungs. Explain that breath is a form of air.
	2. Ask the child to hold her hand near her mouth as she lets the air out, and to describe what it feels like.
Small piece of paper	3. Suggest that she blow on a piece of paper to see her air power.
	4. Ask her to blow on hot food or on her wet hand to determine the cooling effect of air.
	5. Remind the child how water dried on the warm pavement when she water-painted (see science [8] — "Water"). Explain how the sun warmed the air, which then had a drying effect. Ask the child to put her wet hand near a warm radiator or furnace outlet, or on sunny cement or pavement to see how long it takes to dry.
Small paper bag	6. Show the child how to blow into a paper bag to fill it with air.
	7. Allow the child to blow into the bag. Twist the bag shut and explain how air filled the space in the bag. Tell the child to hit the bag hard with her fist to hear the bang as the air escapes.

Small balloon or plastic bag; elastic band or string

8. Help the child blow up a balloon. Secure the end firmly with elastic or string. Explain how air has lightened the balloon. Suggest that the child toss it around to see it float.

Paper straw, spool, or any tubular item; soapy water; few drops of glycerine (optional)

9. Show the child how to blow bubbles through a tube, using soapy water.
10. Explain how the air from her lungs makes the bubbles.
11. Have her toss them in the air to watch them float.

Additional or More Difficult Activities

1. Wind is air
   a. Compare the wind to the breath.
   b. Watch with the child when it is windy outside to see how things are blown about.

   Handkerchief, scarf, or strip of fabric

   c. Take the child outside, holding the handkerchief. Let her watch as the wind moves it.

   Inflated balloon or plastic bag; string

   d. Tie the string to the inflated balloon or bag.
   e. Suggest that the child run with it to watch it for the effect of her moving it through the air.

   Small paper bag; string about two inches long

   f. Give her a paper bag that has a small hole near the top to which a string has been attached. Suggest that she run against the wind and watch the bag open as it fills with air.
2. Wind toys

Plane

Square piece of paper; paper clip (optional)

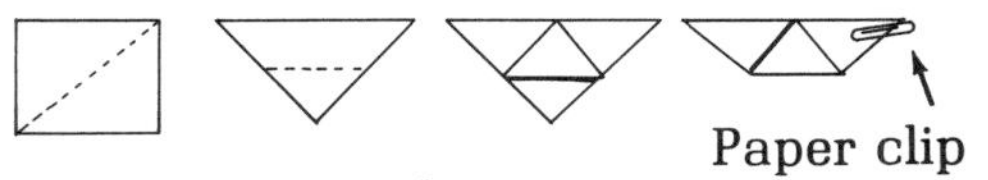

Plane

a. Make a plane by folding the paper in half diagonally (forms a triangle). Fold back from apex end on each side. Attach the paper clip to the nose (see illustration in opposite column).
b. Suggest that the child fly the plane in and out of doors to see what happens in and out of wind.

Pinwheel

Square piece of paper; pencil (unsharpened) or stick; pin or small nail

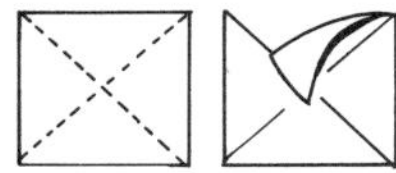
Pinwheel

a. Cut paper in four sections diagonally toward center, leaving half an inch uncut.
b. Fold one corner of each section (every other point) into center, overlapping beyond center a bit.
c. Pin center of pinwheel to a pencil or stick.
d. Ask the child to blow along the edge of the pinwheel, or take it outside on a windy day.
e. Ask her to watch to see what happens as the wind or her breath moves the pinwheel.

Parachute

Small square of cloth; four pieces of string (about twelve inches each); spool or any small item (for weight)

Cloth
String
Weight
Parachute

a. Attach the strings to the four corners of the cloth and then around the weight.
b. Encourage the child to experiment by dropping the parachute from different heights.
c. Tell her to watch the air inflate the cloth.
d. Whenever possible, provide the child with opportunities to experiment with air (with kites, whistles, watching the air ripple the top of water, and so forth).

Suggested age range: Three to five years

(10) Temperature — Hot and Cold

Purpose: To recognize and be able to describe variances in temperature

Concepts

1. Temperature is the degree of hotness or coldness.
2. Everything can be described according to its temperature.

Skills

1. Discrimination
2. Comparison
3. Reasoning

Vocabulary

degree	thermometer	temperature
mercury	hot	cold
warm		

Materials Needed	*Suggested Activities*
	1. Explain to the child that the temperature of everything concerns how hot or cold it is.
	2. Ask him to feel his neck, then yours, and have him feel other things (the cat or dog, inside the refrigerator, the window pane, the floor) to compare the differences.
Thermometer (weather or fever)	3. Show him a thermometer and explain how temperature can be measured. Explain that mercury inside rises when it is warmed and falls when it is cooled.
	4. Whenever you use your oven, explain how it can be set for certain temperatures.
Cooking thermometer	5. If you have a meat or candy thermometer, show the child how mercury (or the hand) moves as the temperature rises and how it falls as the mercury is cooled.
	6. Talk about the temperature of the weather.
	7. Take the child outside for a few minutes, then back inside. Ask him to describe the differences in the temperature that he felt.

Additional or More Difficult Activities

Paper plate or cardboard square; brass paper fastener; felt pen; scissors

Temperature chart

1. Temperature chart
   a. Each morning, encourage the child to check with you to see what the temperature is outside by reading a weather thermometer, watching television, listening to the radio, or reading the weather report in a newspaper.
   b. Make a temperature chart (as shown in column opposite).
   c. Ask the child to mark the temperature on the chart by helping him point the arrow to the correct section.
   d. As the temperature changes during the day, ask him to move the arrow accordingly.

Large zipper (the larger, the better); stapler, tape, or glue; felt pen; cardboard

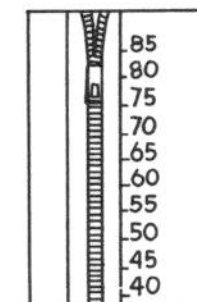

Zipper thermometer

2. Homemade thermometer
   a. Mount a large zipper firmly on a piece of cardboard, on a door, or on a wall.
   b. Show the child how to move the zipper up and down to indicate temperature changes. Help him find the correct numbers after you have determined what the temperature is.
   c. Keep the activity simple enough for him to understand it, but have him check the temperature several times a day and readjust his zipper thermometer each time.

Paper doll and doll clothes (homemade or commercial) or flannel dolls and doll clothes

3. What should I wear?
   a. Talk over with the child the appropriate clothing for various temperatures.
   b. Encourage him to dress the doll each morning after he knows the day's temperature, with appropriate changes during the day.
   c. Ask him to select his own clothes for the same reasons.

Cardboard or paper; scissors; paste or glue; old magazines, catalogs, or newspapers

4. Temperature scrapbook
   a. Make a scrapbook (see mathematics [5] — "Finding Things That Go Together"). Divide it into sections marked "Hot," "Warm," "Cold," and "Cool."
   b. Encourage the child to find pictures of things which show temperature (steaming food, snow scenes, cold drinks in icy glasses, and so on).
   c. Help the child cut out the pictures and paste them in the correct sections of the scrapbook.
   d. Next, ask the child to find pictures of appropriate clothing for each section. Proceed as above.
   e. Discuss the temperature with the child as often as possible.

Mathematics

(1)	Number Concepts	Find Out How Many
(2)	Number Concepts	Learning Numerals
(3)	Ordinal Sequence	What Do We Do?
(4)	Comparison of Number Amounts	Are There More or Less?
(5)	Pairing and Matching	Finding Things That Go Together
(6)	Geometric Shapes	What Is It?
(7)	Time	What Time Is It?
(8)	Conservation of Numbers	Do Both Sets Have the Same Number of Things?
(9)	Relationship of Size to Volume	Which Holds More?
(10)	Length	Who Is the Tallest?

Suggested age range: Three to five years

(1) Number Concepts

Find Out How Many

Purpose: To learn the amounts "1" to "10"

Concepts

1. Amount of objects can be counted and identified by a number name.
2. The progressive order is "1" to "10."

Skills

1. Ability to count from one to ten
2. Recognition of correct number of objects from one to ten
3. Ability to match numbers of objects to a card with a similar number
4. Ability to state the correct number name for different amounts of objects

Vocabulary

one (1)	two (2)	three (3)
four (4)	five (5)	six (6)
seven (7)	eight (8)	nine (9)
ten (10)	count	numbers

Materials Needed

Heavy paper, cardboard (backs of cereal boxes), or any stiff and firm materials; identical small items (snaps, buttons, sticks); additional small items that can be used for matching (toothpicks, bottle caps, toys, bits of colored paper); glue or paste, or needle and thread

Suggested Activities

1. Prepare a set of ten number cards by cutting identically shaped and sized cards (about five by eight inches), or use index cards (commercial).
2. On each card, paste or sew small items: one item on the first card, two items on the next, three items on the next, and so on, until ten items are on the last card.
3. Explain to the child that the "game" is to select the proper number of loose objects and match them correctly to the card with a similar number of objects.
4. Suggest that the child arrange the cards in numerical order before starting.
5. Encourage him to name the numbers and count out loud as he is working.
6. Have him practice this until he is sure of the numerals and their proper sequence.

Additional or More Difficult Activities

1. Counting
   a. Have the child match objects correctly to the number

cards when they are placed out of sequence. Then ask him to put them into proper sequence.

b. Take a tour of the room and ask the child to count how many chairs there are, how many pictures, how many window panes, and so forth.

c. Have him count how many people are in the family (grandparents are legal if he's an only child), how many are in a neighbor's family, and so on.

d. Encourage him to count objects of a similar nature wherever he sees them (cups on the table, bottles of milk in the refrigerator, cans of tuna on the shelf, and so forth).

Empty pail, basket, or grocery bag (barrell type with top folded down); buttons or other small items that can be tossed

2. Button toss

a. Measure a line a foot or two from the pail or grocery bag to a point from which the child will toss the buttons into the pail. Give him from five to twenty buttons to throw, one at a time. Start with five, then add more as he becomes more accurate at this.

b. Each time, after he has thrown the buttons, have him count how many went in the pail. This number becomes his score.

Large sheet of paper; pencil or crayon; scissors; glue

3. What can I do?

a. Ask the child to tell you the things he can do (clap hands, hop on one foot, jump, and the like). List these things on a large sheet of paper.

b. Ask the child to do one of these things and have him count the number of times he does it before tiring.

c. If he can, have him write his scores himself. If he cannot yet write, have him make corresponding number of crayon marks for his score, or cut out and paste the correct number of paper scraps to indicate his daily score.

Paper or cardboard; crayon or felt pen

4. Footprints

a. From heavy paper or cardboard, cut out traced footprints, five for his left foot and five for his right foot.

b. On right footprints, write (in bright red crayon) the even numbers (2, 4, 6, 8, and 10). On left footprints, write in green the odd numbers (1, 3, 5, 7, and 9).

c. Place them in their proper sequence on the floor, spaced so that he can step on them.

d. Let the child step on the proper footprints while saying the proper numbers.

e. Mix them up and have the child say the numbers as he steps on them in mixed order.

f. Hide the footprints round the room and tell him to look for them and place them in their correct order.

Shoebox lid or other box lids; shoelaces or string; macaroni or beads; paper punch

5. Number lacing

a. Punch ten holes in the box lid and write the numbers 1 to 10 beside each hole.

b. Attach a shoelace or a piece of string to each hole.

c. Have the child string the lace or string with the appropriate number of pieces of macaroni or beads (to correspond with the number on the lid).

Tags or cardboard squares (four by four inches); crayon or felt pen; large paper clips

6. Match with clips

a. Cut ten squares of paper and mark each from 1 to 10.

b. Have the child attach as many paper clips to each square as the number printed on the square.

MATH

Suggested age range: Three to five years

(2) Number Concepts

Learning Numerals

Purpose: To recognize numerals

Concepts

1. Identification of numeral symbols
2. The progressive order of numerals

Skills

1. Recognition of each numeral on an individual basis
2. Comprehension of numerals in sequence

Vocabulary

numeral, in order, zero, matching, section

Materials Needed	*Suggested Activities*
Cardboard or any stiff or firm material (sandpaper numeral mounted on cardboard is good — see diagram); paste; scissors	1. Prepare a set of numerals from 1 to 10. These will be prepared in the shape of block numerals and will be mounted on heavy paper or cardboard.

2. Make them about two and a half inches high, three-fourths inch wide, and one-third inch thick. Be sure that the number "10" is made with the two parts attached to form one unit.
3. Ask the child to trace over the numerals with her finger. Encourage her to name the numerals as she traces them.
4. Place the numerals in order. Discuss their names and their order with the child until she seems to know them. Suggest that she handle the numerals herself.
5. Ask the child to place the numerals in order.
6. Hold one numeral behind you to see if the child knows which one is missing. Repeat this until you have hidden all of the numerals, one at a time. Then repeat it by hiding two at a time; then three at a time.
7. Suggest that the child do the hiding.

Block numerals

Additional or More Difficult Activities

Cardboard; scissors; paste or needle and thread; felt pen or crayon; small objects (buttons, snaps); numerals from first activity

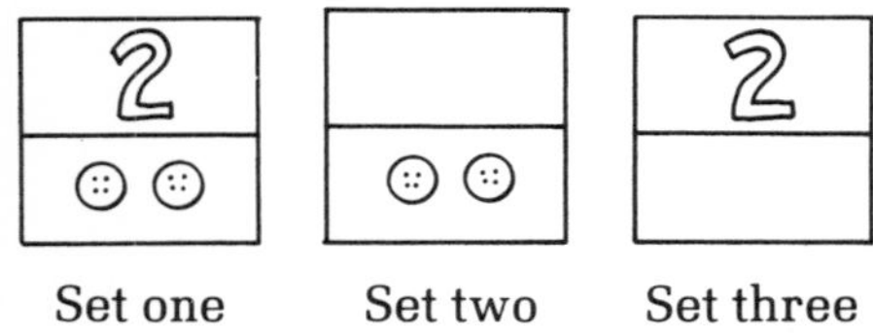

1. Matching numerals
   a. Make three sets of numeral cards (about four by six inches).
   b. Divide one card in half horizontally by drawing a line across the center of the card. On the top half, print a numeral; on the bottom, paste or sew a matching amount of objects (this will be known as "set one").
   c. On set two, proceed as above, leaving the top half blank, but pasting or sewing the same amount of items onto the card.
   d. On set three, print the numeral, but leave the bottom half blank.
   e. Using set one, ask the child to match the numerals and small objects to the cards.
   f. Using set two, ask her to match the numerals to each card.
   g. Using set three, ask her to match the small objects to each card.
   h. Using any of the sets, place the cards at random. Ask her to place them in proper order and then match the appropriate numerals or objects.

Eggbox; small items; set of numerals

2. Eggbox numerals
   a. Cut off the final two cups from an egg carton, leaving ten sections.
   b. Write the numbers 1 to 5 in one row and the numbers 6 to 10 in the other row.
   c. Ask the child to match the block numerals (from the first game) to the correct sections of the eggbox.
   d. Ask her to place the correct number of small items in each section.

Different small objects (such as one clip, two pebbles, three beans) in sets of one to ten

   e. Ask the child to sort into piles the handful of different items you have ready for this activity.
   f. Next ask her to count each of the sorted piles.
   g. Then have her match the piles of objects, according to their numbers, to the proper number section in the box.

3. Zero
   a. Use a blank card and a card you have prepared with a zero (0) printed on the top half.
   b. Show her that the full blank card and the bottom of the card with 0 on it are the same.
   c. When she has placed all of the objects in the eggbox in 2g above, ask her to place the zero card where the objects had been.

Suggested age range: Three and a half to five years

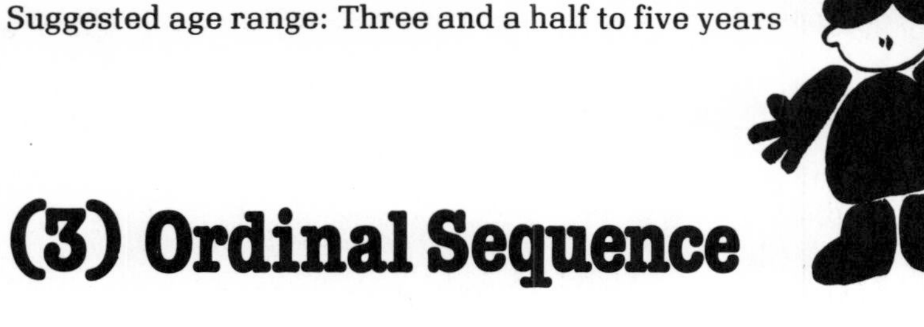

(3) Ordinal Sequence What Do We Do?

Purpose: To be aware of the ordinal names of activities that usually take place in an orderly fashion

Concept: Sequential order of behavior, events, and objects

Skills
1. Comprehension of the order of events
2. Ability to identify and place things in sequential order

Vocabulary

first	second	third
fourth	fifth	sixth (and so on)

Materials Needed	*Suggested Activities*
Pictures of people or animals doing things	1. As the child is involved in doing something (such as washing his face), discuss with him the steps he is taking ("First you roll up your sleeves; second, you turn on the water," and so forth). 2. Ask the child to describe the steps he took when he just did something (you may have to help him recall). 3. Encourage him to use the words "first," "second," "third," and so on. 4. Using pictures, ask the child to describe the steps he imagines the people in the pictures took to do what they are pictured doing ("First, the man came out of the house; second, he got the lawnmower from the garage; third, he started the motor." Or, "First the dog came out of the barn; second, he saw the cow; third, he barked at the cow").

Additional or More Difficult Activities

Three cups, empty cans, food cartons, or other suitable containers; small object (thimble, screw, bolt)

1. Under which?
   a. Using three containers, turn them upside down.
   b. With the child not watching, place the small object under the middle cup.
   c. Ask the child to guess which cup he thinks the thimble is under — the first, second, or third.
   d. After he tells you his guess, let him check by lifting the cups in sequence, reciting "first," "second," as he goes.
   e. Repeat this activity, hiding the thimble in a different place each time.
   f. Let the child hide the object for you to guess.

Egg carton (prepared with ten numbers as before), with small items nestled in each section

2. Which section?
   a. Ask the child to describe what is in each section, using correct ordinal terms: "In the fourth section, there are four elastic bands." Or "In the first section, there is a penny."
   b. Have him fill the sections with items for you to describe.

Several cans of food or several small toys

3. First, second, third
   a. Place the canned food (or toys) in a row.
   b. Ask the child to describe them, using the correct ordinal numbers: "First, there's a can of milk; second, there's a can of dog food; third, there's a can of corn," and so on. Or, "First there's a golf ball; second, there's a rubber duck; third, there's a car," and so forth.
   c. Have the child rearrange the cans or toys and let you describe them. Make a mistake to see if he catches it.

Suggested age range: Three and a half to five years

(4) Comparison of Number Amounts

Are There More or Less?

Purpose: To be able to determine more (greater) than or less than mathematically

Concept: Numbers of amounts are comparative.

Skill: Ability to total amounts or numbers of objects or people and compare them

Vocabulary

more than	greater than	less than
fewer than	compare	comparison

Materials Needed	*Suggested Activities*
Any familiar household objects	1. Discuss with the child how many people will be at the family dinner (supper) table. Give her one less fork than she will need to help you set the table.
	2. Ask the child: "Are there more forks or less forks than there are people?"
	3. Discuss the number of males and females in the family. Ask her, "Are there more boys than girls in our family?"
	4. Compare windows (or doors) in two different rooms. Ask: "Are there fewer windows in the kitchen than in the bedroom?"
Number cards prepared for mathematics (1) — "Find Out How Many"	5. Select the number "4" card and say, "I have four buttons on this card." Then point to the "1" card and ask, "Are there more or less buttons on the number four card?"

Additional or More Difficult Activities

Old magazines, newspapers, or catalogs; scissors

1. Compare
   a. Find different pictures that show similar objects in different quantities.
   b. Show them to the child and compare the numbers of things in each picture.
   c. Encourage her to talk about what she sees; using the correct vocabulary words.
   d. Mix up the pictures and ask the child to compare them for herself, telling you what her comparisons are.
   e. Cut out a new picture, give it to the child, and ask her to find another picture that shows *fewer* objects ("You had three dogs and I have two cars").
   f. Have her find a picture that has *more* objects ("You had three dogs and I have five flags").
   g. Look out the window (or go for a walk with the child), watching for cars and trucks, or cars and bicycles, or cars and people walking. Have her tell you which were *more than* and which were *less than*.
   h. Talk with the child about familiar things, such as her stockings, pajamas, doll, family car. Have her compare which of these are made up of *more* or *less* parts.

Suggested age range: Three and a half to five years

(5) Pairing and Matching

Finding Things That Go Together

Purpose: To be able to pair or match things that are identical or have like qualities

Concepts

1. Many things come in pairs.
2. Many objects are paired to be of most use.

Skills

1. Observation
2. Ability to determine what things can be paired
3. Ability to analyze why things that are dissimilar but have like qualities can be used together

Vocabulary

pair — match — go together

Materials Needed	*Suggested Activities*
Two identical items (such as spoons, pencils, or buttons); paper bag	1. Divide the pairs of items, putting one on the floor in front of the child and the other in a paper bag.
	2. Ask the child to take an item from the bag and try to find the one it matches.
	3. Ask the child to count the number in each set. Explain that the two in every set are called a "pair."
	4. Next, ask him to help sort clothing to be laundered or folded, or have him help pick up clothing, shoes, or other items. Talk about how many things that we wear are called "pairs" (such as pants, socks, shoes, boots, and so on).
Large piece of paper (newspaper can be used); crayons or pencil	5. Ask the child to lie on the floor on a large piece of paper (or several smaller pieces taped together). Draw an outline of his body. Discuss with him how our bodies are made of many pairs.
	6. Help him fill in (with crayons) all the parts of the body of which there are two: eyes, ears, hands, feet, legs, arms, and so on.
	7. Question him: "Do you have one or two mouths?" "How many eyebrows do you have?"
Books, magazines, or catalogs	8. Ask the child to find pictures of *pairs* of things.

Related items (such as comb and brush, knife and fork, cup and saucer, sock and shoe)

9. Help the child learn about the relationship of objects by discussing things that go together. Discuss combinations of objects, such as a knife and a fork.

10. Mix up the related items and ask him to match them.

11. Ask him to set the table. Tell him to put together the objects that match.

Additional or More Difficult Activities

Looseleaf notebook or paper; rings or string; hole puncher; old magazines or newspapers; scissors; paste

Yes match No match

1. Yes and no matches
   a. Make a looseleaf scrapbook. Cut the pages in half horizontally. Cut out six to ten sets of pictures of things that go together. Paste one of the pair on a top half-sheet; the other, on the bottom half-sheet. When all pairs are pasted in in this manner, mix them up when inserting sheets in the notebook.
   b. Ask the child to match the pairs, one at a time, by turning the bottom sheets until he finds the object that matches the picture on the top half.

Twelve items that can be paired (stamp and envelope, teabag and cup, doll and doll bed, flower and vase, bar of soap and wash cloth, jeans and a belt); an additional six unrelated items (pencil, dish towel, toy truck, pillow, magazine, handkerchief)

2. One does not match
   a. Do not let the child watch as you assemble six sets of items with an additional six items that do not match or cannot be paired with any of the sets. For example, a stamp and envelope go together, but a pillow does not belong to this set.
   b. Mix all of the items up and ask the child to find the six pairs that match.
   c. When he has finished matching the items, have him tell you the reasons that he selected some and rejected others for each set.

Old magazines, catalogs, or newspapers; paste; scissors; paper

3. Two match — one doesn't
   a. Cut out six to ten sets of items that can be paired and paste each on a separate piece of paper.
   b. Cut out six to ten single items of unmatching items and paste them on separate pieces of paper.
   c. Proceed as in 2 above, allowing the child to match the pairs and add one that doesn't match.

Suggested age range: Two and a half to four
and a half years

(6) Geometric Shapes — What Is It?

Purpose: To be able to recognize geometric shapes in many settings

Concepts

1. Almost everything has the property of shape.
2. The most common shapes are: a circle, a square, a triangle, and a rectangle.

Skills

1. Recognition of different shapes
2. Ability to describe shapes
3. Ability to see shapes in things, such as the square screen on the television set

Vocabulary

circle	round	square
triangle	rectangle	angle
side	corner	point

Materials Needed

Paper (wrapping, construction, or bags); four milk cartons (or cracker or tissue boxes); scissors; paste

Circle Square Triangle Rectangle

Books, magazines, or catalogs

Suggested Activities

1. Cut out a large assortment of four shapes (see opposite column).
2. Paste one shape on each of the four boxes.
3. Introduce one shape at a time. Ask the child to match it to similar shapes you have made.
4. Next, have her match it to similarly shaped objects in the room (if a circle, match it to a door knob or the round base of a vase).
5. Next, have her match it to similarly shaped objects found in pictures.
6. After she has learned the four shapes, mix all of them together and ask her to sort the shapes into the appropriately labeled boxes.

Additional or More Difficult Activities

Colored paper

1. Sorting shapes
   a. Cut out more sets of shapes of different sizes, using different colors for each set.
   b. Ask the child to sort the shapes by size and then by color.

2. Shape walk
   a. Take the child on a "shape" walk.
   b. Concentrate on one shape in one room at a time.
   c. Let her hold the paper shape in her hand as she looks. Ask, "Can you see something round by the door? Something that looks like your circle?"
   d. Help her by asking, "Do you think the door is shaped like a circle or a rectangle?"

Typing paper or paper bags cut to the approximate size, or wrapping paper; needle and thick thread or wool; old magazines or newspapers; paste

3. Shape booklet
   a. Make a "shape" booklet with your child.
   b. Help her find pictures in magazines or newspapers that represent the four shapes. Plan to have several pages for each shape, first drawing each shape on the top of the page.
   c. Help her cut out and paste the shapes she finds on the appropriate pages.

Paper; crayon or felt pen

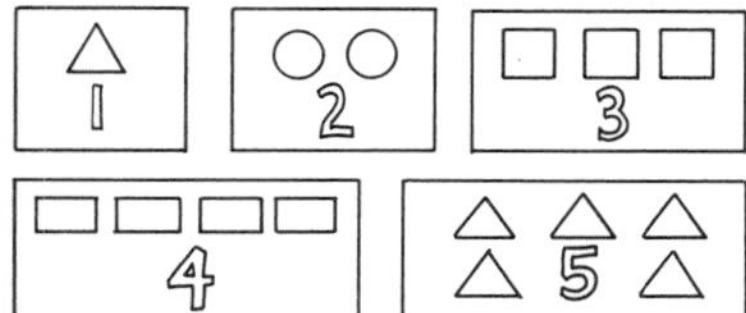

4. Count the shapes
   a. Make a counting book of shapes (see illustration in opposite column).
   b. Let her watch and call out the names of the shapes and how many are on each page as you make them.
   c. Use this activity often to help her review numbers as well as shapes.

Rope, yarn, or string; straws, popsicle sticks, or twigs

5. Make your own shapes
   a. Use either the rope, yarn, or string or the popsicle sticks, straws, or twigs to outline the four shapes.
   b. See if the child can give the names of the shapes as you and she make them.
   c. Ask her to make the shapes by herself.

Heavy paper or cardboard; crayon; differently shaped items (can, jar lid, box, small pad)

6. Tracing shapes
   a. Help the child make shapes by drawing around the differently shaped objects.
   b. Let her color in the shapes and then help her cut them out.
   c. Suggest that she paste them into her shape booklet.

Suggested age range: Three and a half to five years

(7) Time — What Time Is It?

Purpose: To start understanding the concept of time and to begin to learn to tell time

Concepts

1. Time can be measured.
2. People organize their lives with time schedules.

Skills

1. Recognition of hour and minute hands
2. Ability to tell time by "o'clock," "half past," "quarter to," and "quarter after"

Vocabulary

o'clock	half past	quarter to
quarter after	minute	hour

Materials Needed	*Suggested Activities*
Paper plate or heavy paper; string, yarn, or brass paper fastener; crayon or felt pen	1. Make a clock from a paper plate or heavy paper. Cut out hour and minute hands and fasten them onto the clock face with string, yarn, or brass fastener. Print these four numbers on the clock face, starting at the top: 12, 3, 6, and 9 and then fill in the other numbers.
	2. Move the hands to 8 o'clock, then tell the child, "When the big hand (minute) is on the twelve and the little hand (hour) is on the eight, it is eight o'clock."
	3. Ask him to practice placing the hands in the eight o'clock position and saying what time they show.
	4. Discuss other important times with the child, such as when he eats breakfast, when his father gets home from work, and so forth.
	5. Help him find those times on his clock by fixing the hands in the proper position. Ask him to practice these settings. Once he seems to understand what he is doing, ask him to set the hands for "the time you eat breakfast," "the time Daddy gets home," and so on.
	6. Ask the child to point to the times he already knows on the real clock. Then suggest that he copy on his clock the position of the hands on the real clock.

7. Discuss with him the correct way to say the time that the real clock shows.

Large sheet of paper; crayon or felt pen

7:30 GET UP
7:45 EAT BREAKFAST
8:00 PLAY OUTSIDE
9:00 PLAY THESE GAMES
7:00 BED TIME

Pedro's day

8. Make a daily schedule, listing the times that are important to the child.
9. Ask him to place the hands of his clock on the times that show when he gets up, when he eats breakfast, when he goes out to play, when it is time for these learning activities, and so forth.
10. Let him do the telling as he practices setting his clock to the schedule.

Additional or More Difficult Activities

Alarm clock, stove timer, or hourglass

1. Time to
   a. An alarm clock, a stove timer, or an hourglass can also help the child understand the time concept ("You have five minutes before bedtime. I'll set the alarm [or put the timer on] so you'll know when five minutes have passed").
   b. Teach the child to use these timers himself so that he can experiment with the different lapses of time.

Television or radio

   c. At station breaks, encourage the child to listen for the announced time, then have him arrange the hands on his clock to that time. Check his clock to help him do this correctly should he make mistakes.

Television or radio time schedules (from newspaper or weekly TV magazine)

   d. Help the child find his favorite programs on the radio or television schedule. Ask him to set the hands on his clock to correspond to the times of his favorite programs.

2. The time it takes
   a. When the child goes out to play, have him check the time on the real clock and mark it with the hands on his clock. When he returns, ask him to do the same things.
   b. Discuss with him the exact times he went out and returned and the time that elapsed in the interval.
   c. When the child starts to do something (get dressed in the morning, color with crayon, play with toys), discuss with him his opinion of how long he thinks it will take.
   d. Ask him to set the timer (or alarm clock) or help him place the hands of his clock at the time he believes he will have finished dressing or coloring.
   e. When he does finish, check the time to see if he took more or less time than he had anticipated.
   f. When he is away from home, encourage him to look at clocks wherever he goes (grocery store, bus depot, airport, movies).

Suggested age range: Four to five years

(8) Conservation of Numbers

Do Both Sets Have the Same Number of Things?

Purpose: To understand that the number of objects in a set remains the same even if placed in different arrangements

Concept: The number of objects remains the same even if they are placed in different arrangements.

Skills

1. Recognition that the number of objects can remain the same even after their positions are changed
2. Ability to count and otherwise discern numbers of objects in different arrangements

Vocabulary

number	set	space
arrangement	remain	scatter
compare		

Materials Needed	*Suggested Activities*
Six identical items (such as oranges, screws, spoons) and six other identical items (such as apples, bolts, forks)	1. Select six identical items (such as oranges) and six other identical items (such as apples) that are the same size. Place the six oranges in a row and ask the child to place the other six (apples) in a row beneath the oranges.
	2. Ask her to count the oranges and then the apples.
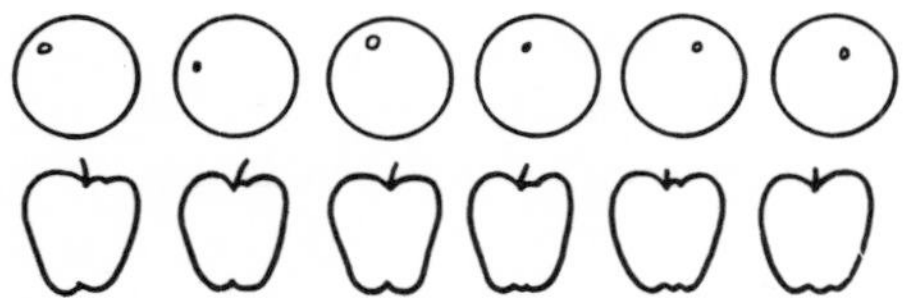	3. Pick up the oranges and place them in a row beneath the apples, but with more space between each one.
	4. Ask the child, "Are there the same number here" (point to the oranges) "as there are here?" (point to the apples).
	5. Use other arrangements to be sure that the child is not using space as a basis for judgment.
	6. Ask her to count the number of oranges and apples each time you make a new arrangement.
	7. Mix them up and ask her to count them and tell you how many oranges and how many apples.

Additional or More Difficult Activities

Twenty buttons or pebbles

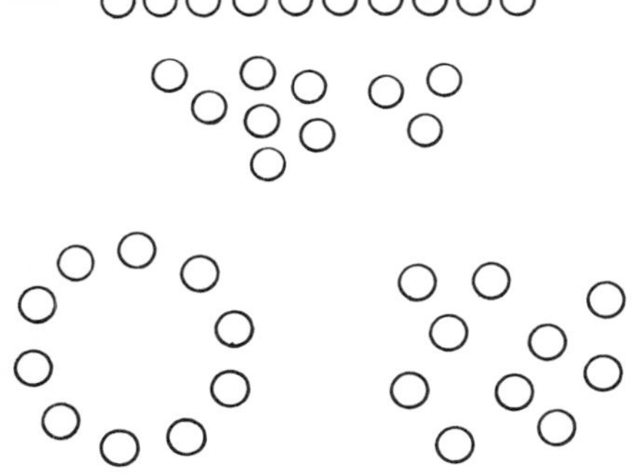

1. Compare
   a. Using twenty buttons or pebbles, place ten in a straight line and scatter the other ten.
   b. Point to the straight line and ask her, "Are there the same number of buttons in this line as there are in this scattered mixture?"
   c. Allow her to count them, and help her if she has difficulty with the scattered ones.
   d. Repeat this several times, varying the positions of the buttons (such as a circle and scattered, a square and a diagonal line).
   e. Let the child arrange the buttons in a straight line (or a circle or square) and the remaining buttons in any manner she wishes. Question her as to the number of buttons each time.

Egg carton; six colored buttons; six white buttons

2. Button eggs
   a. Place one colored button in each of the six sections on one side of the egg carton. Ask the child to count the buttons.
   b. Pick up one of the buttons and place it in the adjoining section (leaving one section empty and one section with two buttons in it). Ask her, "Now are there the same number of buttons?"
   c. If she answers correctly, place six white buttons on the other side of the egg carton, one in each section, and ask, "Are there the same number of white buttons as colored buttons?"
   d. Repeat this several times, varying the position of the buttons and asking the child to compare the number of buttons each time.
   e. Mix the white and colored buttons, some sections empty and some with two or three buttons in them. Ask the child to count to see if there are the same number of buttons each time.
   f. Allow the child to mix them up and then count them again. Each time, ask her to compare the number of white and the number of colored buttons.

Suggested age range: Three and a half to five years

(9) Relationship of Size to Volume

Which Holds More?

Purpose: To determine the amount that small and large containers can hold

Concepts

1. Objects can be described as small and large.
2. Small containers hold less (or a smaller volume of contents) than larger containers.
3. Large containers hold more (or a larger [greater] volume of contents) than smaller containers.

Skills

1. Observation
2. Ability to speculate
3. Ability to experiment

Vocabulary

small	large	size
volume	holds	full
to fill	to empty	equal
enough	more (or greater) than	not enough
container		

Materials Needed	*Suggested Activities*
One small and one large clear container (as identical as possible), such as plastic glasses, bottles, or boxes (clear food bags can be used, but they are harder for the child to handle); bag of dried beans or macaroni, or buttons; sand or dirt; measuring cup; water	1. Show the containers to the child. Discuss their sizes with him and ask him to name them correctly ("big glass," "little glass"). Encourage him to say "small glass" and "large glass." 2. When he understands the size differences, give him the beans or macaroni to fill each container, then let him empty them. Discuss with him what is happening in relation to the volume of each container and the amount of beans it will hold. 3. Measure and fill each container with an equal amount of beans. Ask the child to note the differences in the filled volume of each container. Talk over with him how he can make the larger container full (by adding more beans).

4. Encourage the child to empty and fill the containers, discussing with him the steps he takes to do this.

5. Guide the child's continued experiments in the use of the buttons, macaroni, sand, dirt, and water for comparing the amounts held by each container.

Additional or More Difficult Activities

1. More comparisons
   a. Suggest that the child look round the house for other container-type objects (boxes, bags, flower pots, doll carriages, toy trucks, empty handbag, and so on).
   b. Ask him to measure out the amounts of beans each holds and then compare their volumes according to the amount of beans needed for each.

Magazines or newspapers

   c. Help the child find and cut out pictures of container-type objects. Ask him to sort them according to small and large. Discuss their volumes with him.

Picture books

   d. As the child looks at pictures, ask him to talk about the different sizes and volumes of the containers he sees.

2. How much do I hold?
   a. Ask the child to note the size of the portions eaten at meals by him, his father, his brothers, and his sisters.
   b. Discuss these amounts in relation to each person's size and the amount of food the person's stomach will probably hold.

3. Volume walk
   a. Take the child for a walk (or this can be done while the family is taking a drive) and talk with him about the many things he sees.
   b. Ask him to speculate about the comparative amount of water, for example, that he thinks each might be able to hold ("See that wheelbarrow and that mailbox? Do you think the mailbox holds more water than the wheelbarrow?").

Suggested age range: Four to five years

(10) Length — Who Is the Tallest?

Purpose: To understand length measurement

Concept: Length is measurable on anything we can see.

Skills

1. Observation
2. Comparison
3. Ability to measure

Vocabulary

tall	long	short
height	high	low
ruler	measure	tape measure
measuring stick (yardstick)		

Materials Needed	*Suggested Activities*
	1. Ask the family members to stand in a row before a full-length mirror. Discuss and compare each's height (be sure to pronounce it correctly — rhymes with night — many mispronounce it with an additional "h" on the end).
	2. Take height measurements of the family members by asking them to stand against a closet door and marking the spot where the tops of their heads reach.
	3. Show the child the different marks and discuss who is taller, shorter, and so on.
Ruler, tape measure, or measuring stick; string; scissors	4. Measure the heights with a ruler, a tape measure, or a measuring stick. Explain to the child what you are doing.
	5. Cut the string in lengths that correspond to the heights of the family members. Stretch these strings on the floor and discuss the differences in length with the child. See if she can guess which strings match the family members' heights.
	6. Mix the strings up and ask the child to sort them from the tallest to the shortest.

Family photographs or pictures in books, magazines, or catalogs

7. Show her pictures of the family or other people and talk to her about their comparative heights. Ask her to compare who is taller (or shorter) than whom ("Uncle Charles is taller than Uncle David, but Daddy is taller than Uncle Charles").

Heavy butcher or wrapping paper; scissors; crayons

8. Ask the child to lie down on a large piece of heavy paper that you have placed on a smooth floor or other surface. Trace around her body. Cut out her silhouette and help her measure the length of the parts of her body.

9. Make similar silhouettes of other children, or of teddy bears or dolls, and have her compare these measurements with hers.

Additional or More Difficult Activities

Tape measure or ribbon

1. Measurements everywhere
   a. Give the child a tape measure or ribbon so that she can measure and compare heights of toys, the car and bike, furniture, books, magazines, pots, pails, and whatever is within reach.

Shadows

2. Shadow measurements
   a. Walk outside on a sunny day. Find a spot where your shadows are easily seen and discuss these with the child. Experiment to make the shadows lengthen (become taller and shorter).
   b. Ask the child to find shadows of trees, shrubs, buildings, and so forth, and talk about what she sees concerning length measurements ("The bush isn't as tall as the tree, but its shadow looks longer because the sun is right behind it now").

Assorted lengths of rope, yarn, string, and ribbon

3. Matching the talls and the shorts
   a. Cut four identical long and four identical short segments from a piece of rope. Give them to the child to match the tall and the short pieces.
   b. Cut out another set of four long and four short (from some other material) and give them to the child also.
   c. Mix rope and other segments and ask the child to match the long and short pieces and then sort the rope pieces from the other pieces.
   d. Cut out and add more sets of different material for the child to sort and match.

Ruler or ribbon segment; picture book of animals

4. Find the tallest and the shortest animals
   a. Give the child a ruler or ribbon cut approximately twelve inches.
   b. Ask her to measure the animals in the pictures and tell you which is the shortest and the tallest.

5. Talls and shorts out of doors
   a. When out for a walk or ride, talk to the child about the length measurements of people, cars, trees, buildings, signs, distant hills, and so forth.
   b. Encourage her to be mindful of short, shorter, and shortest and of tall, taller, and tallest in all she sees.

Appendix A

Suggested Reading for Parents

Parent-Child Relationships and Child Development

Briggs, Dorothy C. *Your Child's Self-Esteem.* Garden City, New York: Doubleday & Company, Inc. 1970

Chess, Stella; *et al. Your Child Is a Person.* New York: The Viking Press, Inc. 1972.

Dodson, Fitzhugh. *How to Parent.* Los Angeles: Nash Publishing Co. 1970.

Spock, Benjamin. *Baby and Child Care.* New York: E. P. Dutton & Co., Inc. 1968.

Home Teaching: How to Do It Books

Arnold, Arnold. *Teaching Your Child to Learn from Birth to School Age.* Englewood Cliffs, New Jersey: Prentice-Hall, Inc. 1971.

Bell, T. H. *Your Child's Intellect.* Salt Lake City: Olympus Publishing Company. 1972.

Cole, Ann; *et al. Learning Together: Creative Activities for the Home.* Northfield, Illinois. 1973.

__________. *Recipes for Fun: Activities to Do at Home with Children.* Northfield, Illinois. 1970.

__________. *More Recipes for Fun.* Northfield, Illinois. 1972.

De Franco, Ellen; and Pickarts, Evelyn. *Dear Parents: Help Your Child to Read.* New York: American Book Company. 1972.

Gordon, Ira J. *Baby Learning through Baby Play.* New York: St. Martin's Press. 1971.

__________. *Child Learning through Child Play.* New York: St. Martin's Press. 1973.

Gregg, Elizabeth. *What to Do When "There's Nothing to Do."* New York: Delacorte Press. 1967.

Marzollo, Jean; and Lloyd, Janice. *Learning through Play.* New York: Harper & Row, Publishers, Incorporated. 1972.

Sharp, Evelyn. *Thinking Is Child's Play.* New York: E. P. Dutton & Co., Inc. 1969.

Appendix B

Sources of Free or Relatively Inexpensive Materials

The Home

Boxes, cartons, tin cans, paper, paper bags, cardboard, tubes from bathroom tissue and paper towels, plastic containers, jars, jar lids, fabric scraps, unmatched socks, spools (thread), yarn, thread, and so forth

Stores and Markets

These include places where items can be purchased or obtained free of charge, such as:

Awning, shades, venetian blinds — fabric scraps, cord, rope

Boatyards — scraps such as wood, metal, rope, sailcloth

Cabinetmakers and carpenters — wood ends in a variety of shapes, sawdust

Camera shops — spools, reels, plastic and tin containers, spoiled film, packing boxes

Carpet, rug, and floor coverings — samples, swatches, discarded sample books, cardboard tubes

Clothing — boxes; wrapping and tissue paper; damaged, unmated, and old stock items

Florist — boxes, plant pots, soft wire, decorative paper and ribbon, plant clippings

Food — boxes, cartons, bags, meat and fruit trays, plastic bag fasteners, excelsior

Furniture — packing boxes, paper, fabric samples

Gas station — inner tubes, discarded tires

Hardware and household appliances — boxes wrapping paper, cardboard, excelsior or shredded packing materials, styrofoam packing boxes, wire, rope, string, old stock items

Ice cream parlor — large empty cartons, containers, plastic spoons

Laundromat and dry cleaner — boxes, large plastic bags, wire hangers, plastic containers

Lumber yard — wood ends, sawdust

Newspaper — unprinted newsprint paper, cardboard tubes

Paint and wallpaper — boxes, cartons, sample sheets, swatches and discarded sample books

Stationery — paper, cardboard, boxes, wrappings

Telephone company — wire and cable scraps, large wooden spools, discarded phones

Upholstery and drapery — swatches, sample books, cardboard tubes, spools, plastic and metal curtain rings, foam rubber

Vending machine companies — boxes, crates, bottle caps

Yarn — yarn ends, large cardboard spools, discarded pattern books

Index